Praise for
The Relational Manager

'The Relational Manager delivers what it promises – a clear, straightforward and pragmatic guide to the importance of relationships at work. It is sensible, well judged and should provide an invaluable guide for busy executives who sometimes forget this central part of their work.'
Rob Goffee, Professor of Organisational Behaviour, London Business School

'When I first encountered the work of the Relationships Foundation, countless events and incidents in organizational settings over many years suddenly made sense. Michael Schluter and David Lee understand how people think and behave. Managing an organization mainly involves managing human beings. Relational thinking is a critical tool for those who aim to be better managers.'
The Hon. Lindsay Tanner MP, Minister for Finance and Deregulation, Australia

'At the heart of every worthwhile activity are people and people thrive on strong relationships. Those leaders who understand this relational agenda are already well on their way to achieving their goals. *The Relational Manager* offers powerful insights and practical actions to help leaders bring out the best in themselves and the people they manage. In a world of stress and sleaze, it has never been more relevant.'
Clive Mather, former Chairman of Shell UK and CEO of Shell, Canada

'One of the most significant assets in any organization is its reputation. Its reputation is built through relationships, maintained through relationships and may even be destroyed through not nurturing relationships. This book will provide any director with valuable guidance to assist in establishing relationships with their stakeholders.'
Lindie Engelbrecht, Chief Executive of the Institute of Directors, South Africa

To Phil, who walks the talk

MICHAEL SCHLUTER
& DAVID JOHN LEE

THE Relational
MANAGER

Transform your workplace AND your life

LION

A Lion Book
an imprint of
Lion Hudson plc
Wilkinson House, Jordan Hill Road,
Oxford OX2 8DR, England
www.lionhudson.com

ISBN 978 0 7459 5368 7 (UK)
ISBN 978 0 8254 7936 6 (US)

Distributed by:
UK: Marston Book Services, PO Box 269, Abingdon, Oxon, OX14 4YN
USA: Trafalgar Square Publishing, 814 N. Franklin Street, Chicago, IL 60610
USA Christian Market: Kregel Publications, PO Box 2607, Grand Rapids, MI 49501

First edition 2009

10 9 8 7 6 5 4 3 2 1 0

A catalogue record for this book is available
from the British Library

Typeset in 11/14 Adobe Caslon Pro
Printed and bound in Malta

In the quantum world, relationships
are not just interesting;
to many physicists, they are all
there is to reality.

Margaret Wheatley

Contents

Acknowledgments

We are much indebted to our wives, Auriel and Loralee, whose support has made the writing possible. We would also like to thank those whose generous financial support helped fund the writing and production of this book, and also the many others who shared with us their expertise or commented on the manuscript. Among these are John Ashcroft, Will Candler, Roy Childs, Gideon Hudson, Nick Isbister, Harvey and Kelly McMahon, Clive Mather, Alison Myers, David Parish, Tim Passingham, Jonathan Rushworth, Paul Sandham, Mark Scholefield, Paul Shepanski, Jonathan Winter and David Wong. A special word of thanks is due to Marilyn Collins, who coordinated communication for the project, and to Stephanie Heald, who first saw the possibility of writing a book of this kind.

Preface

At the beginning of the 1990s, we began to discuss a book on relationships. What finally emerged from that discussion was a book called *The R Factor* – a fairly substantial work on political economics.

What we proposed was a simple but radical idea. Society is a network of relationships, private and professional. If those relationships don't work, quality of life goes down and organizational performance suffers. Consequently, it's in everybody's interest to make sure that relationships work well.

We set out to show just how far-reaching the effects of poor relationships are, and put forward a framework for a 'relationships approach' to policy-making and management.

The book gave rise to a Cambridge-based 'think and do tank' called the Relationships Foundation. Since the publication of *The R Factor* in 1993, the Relationships Foundation has developed a number of major initiatives, showing that a 'relationships approach' is effective in policy areas as diverse as criminal justice, healthcare and tackling unemployment. (For more information, see www.relationshipsfoundation.org.)

The extensive research and praxis of the Relationships Foundation provides the core thinking behind *The Relational Manager*.

The world 'relationships' is now in widespread use among those who write about management. As it becomes harder to differentiate products, so more emphasis is placed on the organization's relationship with the customer, on productive teamwork and on helping staff to resolve tensions between the worlds of work and life.

What nobody has done is place all this thinking on a simple, understandable and practical premise. We believe that the relationships approach outlined in this book constitutes a genuinely new way of going about the job of management.

Astute readers will notice that in a number of places we have drawn on our earlier work, published by the Relationships Foundation, entitled *The R Option*.

Directly and indirectly, many people have contributed to the ideas in these pages. We acknowledge them all. Any errors or deficiencies remain the sole property of the authors.

Michael Schluter and David John Lee

About the Authors

Michael Schluter

Michael Schluter studied Economics and Economic History at Durham University. He then did a PhD in Agricultural Economics at Cornell University in the USA, which involved eighteen months of fieldwork in India, based at the Indian Institute of Management in Ahmedabad. He lived in Kenya from 1974 to 1982, working first as a manager for a local company setting up rural industries and then as a research fellow with the International Food Policy Research Institute and as a consultant economist with the World Bank.

He returned to the UK in 1982 to establish the Jubilee Centre as a Christian think tank. In 1985, he brought together a coalition of retailers, unions, churches and other religious leaders to form the Keep Sunday Special Campaign which, in 1986, famously inflicted on Margaret Thatcher her only total defeat on a bill in the House of Commons. Following that, he helped to facilitate confidential meetings between leading members of the South African establishment and the black leadership, including the ANC, between 1987 and 1991.

He is now Chief Executive of Relationships Global, established in 2009, which seeks to promote the relationships approach in organizations and at a policy level across the world.

In addition, he is Life President of City*life*, an Industrial and Provident Society set up by the Relationships Foundation to develop innovative city-based responses to unemployment and urban regeneration, and policy adviser to Concordis, an international peace charity.

Michael Schluter lives in Cambridge, UK. He is married

with three grown-up children who are all heavily into family management. In his spare time (of which he admits he has very little), he enjoys watching rugby and reading history.

David John Lee

David John Lee graduated in Geography from Oxford University. He then studied Theology at Regent College, Vancouver, before returning to the UK to take up a career in writing and publishing, based in Cambridge, London and St Andrews.

He has collaborated with Michael Schluter on a number of projects. His own books include *Ex Machina*, a collection of theatre scripts, and *Doomsday: the Survivor's Guide*, the only title released by HarperCollins UK for the Millennium. He has performed at the Edinburgh Festival Fringe and run a widely acclaimed exhibition that combined the best creative talents of the UK's leading advertising agencies, including Saatchi & Saatchi and Abbott Mead Vickers.

In 2001, the Haggai Institute for Advanced Leadership Training appointed him as their senior writer, a position in which he works with top organizational leaders from over 180 nations. He has a broad creative brief covering writing and publishing, web design, animation, multimedia presentation and show design.

He and his wife Loralee have a special relationship with India, where they have many friends and from where they have adopted their three daughters. They moved to France in 2003 and currently live in the French Alps.

Relational Thinking

Think of one thing you do in management that *doesn't* involve relationships.

It's not easy.

Budgets are numbers – but they also represent a set of decisions about the relative priority of tasks and thus affect relationships with, and within, your team.

Workflow is a PowerPoint slide with boxes and arrows – but it defines responsibilities and expectations in the relationships between team members.

Reporting may require an afternoon alone with your laptop – but what you report will affect your relationship with senior management.

Being a manager is an intrinsically *relational* activity. Coordinating, cooperating and competing are all *relational* actions. Your job pretty much shakes down into a set of connections (with colleagues, consultants, suppliers and customers) in which you progress by performing a range of *relational* tasks – motivating, meeting others' needs, incentivizing, negotiating, resolving conflict, cultivating talent and generally 'getting along with people'.

Much the same could be said of life outside the workplace. Relationships are just fundamental – so fundamental, in fact, that we often pay little attention to them. Which is why, like most managers, you probably haven't considered that 'thinking relationally' – about your organization and how it works – might unlock some of the most pressing dilemmas you face, both inside the workplace and outside it.

Take a one-minute test

Here's a place to start.

Look at these five groups of people you're connected to and make a snap assessment of your relationships in each group. Is there enough trust and confidence in the relationships? Is there enough time to devote to them? Is there enough practical support going on? And is there enough agreement?

In each case, you have two options: either DOING OK or COULD BE BETTER.

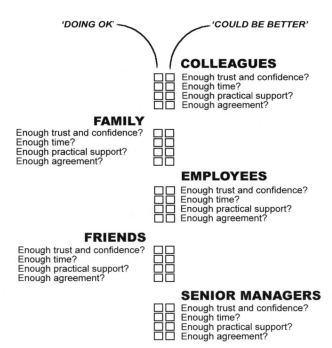

DIAGRAM 1: A one-minute relationship assessment

After sixty seconds it will have struck you that relationships are more complex than they appear.

For example, the qualities you're assessing are often *directional*.

Who is *getting* the practical support? Who is providing it? And should it all be going one way or not?

And there's a lot at stake in that word 'enough'. Although we are reluctant to admit we're *not* DOING OK, we also hesitate to confirm we're receiving *enough* of the things that good relationships are supposed to provide. Anyway, 'enough' seems to mean different things, depending on which relationship you're talking about. What exactly is 'enough time' with your senior manager, with your partner, with your 2i/c and with your friends?

At this point, many will throw their hands up and say, 'I take what I can get. And anyway, there's not much I can do about it.'

But that is exactly the point. No matter where you are in the management structure and no matter what kind of organization you work in, you have extensive control over the relationships on which you and your organization depend. A relationships approach to management will affect almost every aspect of your life and work. You just need the tools to work with.

The soft issues are the hard issues

A study in the USA has shown that about 40 per cent of new management recruits fail within the first eighteen months. The study concludes: 'Failure to build good relationships with peers and subordinates is the culprit an overwhelming 82 per cent of the time.'[1]

This is just one statistic from a mounting stack of evidence – both academic and anecdotal – that relationships are crucial to businesses and organizations. They matter vitally at four levels.[2]

1. At a strategic level

All business organizations search for competitive advantage.

But, viewed objectively, a product may not be easy to differentiate from its rivals. Motorists do not usually think of petrol bought at a Shell station as qualitatively different from petrol of the same type bought at a BP station. Nor is taste necessarily what motivates a consumer to buy Heineken lager rather than Stella Artois lager.

Getting a larger slice of a market, then, may depend heavily on branding.

Brand is a relational concept because it is all about trust between the company and the consumer. The trust relates to the quality of the product and the service attached to it. A brand is a promise. There are 'moments of truth' that are critical for how people view a brand and whether they believe in it. For example, when a person rings up with a complaint, how are they treated?

Advertising often gives brands relational content. Coca-Cola commercials have often tried to create associations between the product and the context in which it is consumed. They have linked relational experiences with the brand, so that what you buy is not a drink with a certain taste and packaging but a drink connected with certain relational events. The route to profit is understood to be relational.

And between the producer and the end-consumer lies a network of relationships that also impact business success. In the words of management guru Robert Waterman, 'The key to strategic success is mainly this: building relationships with customers, suppliers, and employees that are exceptionally hard for competitors to duplicate.'[3] Unlike products, relationships are tough to replicate quickly. You can't buy them in. And as a result, what might be called the 'relational architecture' a business has built up over the years is its primary source of competitive advantage.

2. At a cultural level

The term 'culture' is used fairly sloppily in business. In fact, culture exists within – and is a quality of – the relationships that hold a business together. The culture can work either for you or against you. It also sets the framework for future relationships, either enabling or constraining them, resulting in either a virtuous or a vicious circle.

When we say that the culture 'is receptive to change', we generally mean that relationships are strong enough to accommodate new patterns of working without a breakdown of trust. Cultures resistant to change almost always reveal weak relationships and low levels of mutual confidence – most notably between various levels of management.

Relationships, then, give us a more precise and useful language to deal with so-called 'cultural' issues. An example of this is provided by Amerco, where, in a workshop for human resource managers, participants explored ways to make friendship work for the benefit of the company – for example, by calling a friend for a chat and asking for help with a work issue.[4]

3. At an operational level

No company can survive without policies, procedures and systems.

But, again, what we are really talking about here is relationships. A system is a relational pattern – a statement of who should relate to whom about what. But that pattern has to be made to work in real relationships between real people. If those people don't get on, no system is going to save you.

Conversely, it's often the case that inadequate, outdated or clumsily applied systems can be made to work if actual working relationships provide the 'lubricating oil'. An American retailer called *The Container Store*, for example, has established some simple operational principles. Among these are 'We treat our employees as humans' and 'Treat people as you want to be treated'. The company also gives its employees full access to the company accounts. The outcome: a company whose staff turnover is a fraction of the industry as a whole.[5]

Relationships form the 'glue' that binds individuals and teams together in an enterprise. Good relationships create efficiencies, trust and motivation. By contrast, an inability to form and maintain good relationships – with customers and suppliers as well as within the enterprise – imposes costs through reduced workflow, diminished morale and lost contracts.

4. At a personal level

For you, the individual manager, it is relationships at the office that make your work either pleasant or intolerable. Overbearing bosses, office politics, bullying, sexual harassment, unhealthy competitiveness between individuals – all these are signs of dysfunction in relationships. And a mismanaged relational environment impacts directly on morale, motivation and productivity. This explains the intense interest shown by top companies in setting up relationships in such a way as to retain their employees.

According to an investigation by *Fortune* in 2000, the 100 'best companies to work for in America' all provide 'a supportive and challenging workplace in which communication is encouraged, ingenuity rewarded, and internal mobility expected' – a situation which is 'maintained by managers who are both visible and accessible'.[6]

What is relational thinking?

Ask most people what 'relational' means when applied to management and they are likely to come up with something in the area of human resources. For example:

◆ someone who pays personal attention to staff

◆ someone who has gone out of his or her way to acquire 'people skills'

◆ someone who realizes that happy employees are less prone to disaffection and militancy.

But these things do not in themselves add up to relational

management. That begins with relational thinking, which in turn begins by breaking out of conventional ways of seeing the world around you.

Consciously or unconsciously, most people absorb information through a filter. For example, most people in business will assess a company through a financial filter. They prioritize the balance sheet. They want to know what's being spent on materials, infrastructure, operations, debt-servicing and payroll, how much turnover results and how much of that turnover goes to profit.

Those concerned about the environment will pick up a different filter. This environmental filter throws up a different set of questions. How much waste does a facility produce? How much water and power does it consume? What are its carbon emissions? How heat efficient are the buildings?

A third kind of assessment would focus on space and ergonomics. Here the key questions would explore the links between layout, location and function. The efficiency of large airports, for example, will be assessed in terms of ease of access, adequate parking, clarity of signage and the effectiveness of procedures that move passengers through check-in, passport control and security.

We will all see different things as significant in a business and ask different questions about it, depending on which of these filters we use to observe it.

In one way, 'relationships' stands alongside things such as 'finance' and 'environment' as another filter through which to assess business organizations. Relationally, we might ask who are the stakeholders involved in a business, how they are connected to others inside and outside the enterprise, what goals, pressures and incentives bear on those relationships, how strong those relationships are and what outcomes result from them.

But note two things.

First, the finances of a company, as well as the impact they make on other categories such as environment and health, depend largely on relationships. To ask how successfully a company markets a product is to ask about the relationships forged between company sales reps and the corresponding buyers. To ask about the risks posed by toxic emissions is to ask about the relationship – or perhaps lack of relationship – between company directors and members of the public who live near the production plant. There is little in business that does not, in the end, hang on the quality of relationships between individuals and among stakeholder groups.

Second, relationships provide a far more comprehensive key to success than finances do. Remuneration may have the advantage that you can write it down on a spreadsheet, but the number in itself has little meaning once you uncouple it from the uses to which that money is put – and those uses are nearly always relational. The pleasure of high earning and the pain of not having enough both impact on us via our relationships. Wealth confers social status, which is an aspect of relationship. Unemployment leads directly to stresses on family and friendships, which are categories of relationship. If it is true that money can't buy happiness, that is because most forms of happiness lie in a relational realm where market rules do not apply.

Love and work

Day after day, the quality of your relationships impacts on the quality of your life. *Relational* events – a disagreement with the boss, a successful negotiation, a great evening out with friends, a child leaving home – will ripple out, deeply affecting your confidence, concentration, work performance and sense of well-being. From a personal as well as a business point of view, there's a big advantage to getting relationships right.

Money cannot substitute for relational well-being. Western cultures tend to muddle money and relationships. A market-driven culture keeps telling us the bottom line is financial. We all have to pay the rent. And most of the opportunities on offer – to travel, dress well, live in pleasant surroundings – have to be bought. But the well-rounded life simply does not consist of unlimited hours at the office and a generous wage settlement. We are happiest when we know we are loved.

How can we use the word 'love' in a business book? Because

life has no joins and seams. Your superlative performance in the workplace rests on relational foundations that fill the whole twenty-four hours of day. Growing up amid supportive and positive relationships, we develop self-esteem. Without those close relationships, we quickly lose our sense of personal security and well-being. And that hits our work.

If relationships go wrong, money can't do much to help. You cannot buy loyalty. You cannot replace a parent with a childminder without courting heartache and disruption. In reality, money itself is only a convenient way of tallying how much one person can ask of another. As everyone in business knows, you can't even make money without effective relationships, because markets and companies are, in the end, only groups of people working together.

Relationships answer our need to understand where we come from and who we are.

According to the former leader of the Life and Work movement, J. H. Oldham:

It is through our responses to other persons that we become persons. It is others who challenge, enlighten and enrich us.

There is no such thing as the isolated individual... Reality is the lived relation. Through sharing in the giving and receiving of mutual being the 'I' becomes real. Reality is an activity in which I share without being able to appropriate it for myself.

Where there is no sharing there is no reality. ... all real life is meeting.[7]

Ways to implement relational thinking

Every chapter in this book examines a different area of relational management and suggests some possible ways to implement relational management in the real world. The subtitle to this book is *Transform your business and your life*, for the simple reason that a relationships approach really cannot be applied piecemeal. To engage with being a relational manager is to engage in the challenge of living a relational life. Life contains business, not the other way around, and many of the constraints on our relationships affect us outside the workplace as much as they do inside it.

So, as an initial exercise, start to map out your worlds – public and private – in terms of relationships and get a feel for the role relationships play. Here are two things you might consider.

1. Chart your 'relational base'

A simple exercise for exploring the relational structures around you begins with drawing up a relational 'radar diagram'. Diagram 2 shows a diagram filled out by an imaginary executive. Diagram 3 is blank for your own use.

The exercise is highly subjective. It's up to you what you rate as a significant relationship – and that's the whole point, because only you can make that judgment. Mark relationships as crosses. Suggest their level of significance in terms of distance from you. The inner circle allows you to distinguish 'significant and close' from 'significant but less close'.

On the business side, include all the main people you have to interact with. These may be team members, superiors, subordinates, clients/customers, suppliers, contractors or peers in other organizations. There's nothing sophisticated about the diagram. It's just a visual device for identifying those working relationships that – for whatever reason – you identify as most important and that contain your source of social support.

You could ask yourself a number of questions. For example, are there any key relationships to which you are not giving enough attention? If so, how can you give more? And how successful are you in prioritizing those relationships that are most important to you?

2. Scan your company with a relational 'filter'

At any level in the organization, you will have some degree of influence on your company's culture, procedures, structure and operations. So, consciously use a relational 'filter' and take a look around. Here are a few questions you might ask about

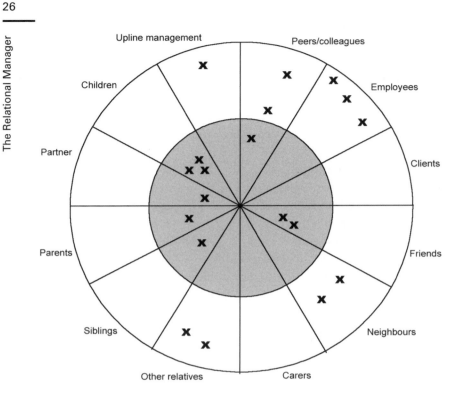

**DIAGRAM 2: A typical relational base. The grey area
shows the person's closest relationships.**

how the company works in relationship terms.

◆ How much meeting takes place between managers and
their teams? How often, where, how regularly, and is there
time for discussion?

◆ Does the staff understand, and buy into, company goals?

◆ How is the annual staff appraisal done?

◆ What provisions does the company make for those with
illness or other emergency difficulties?

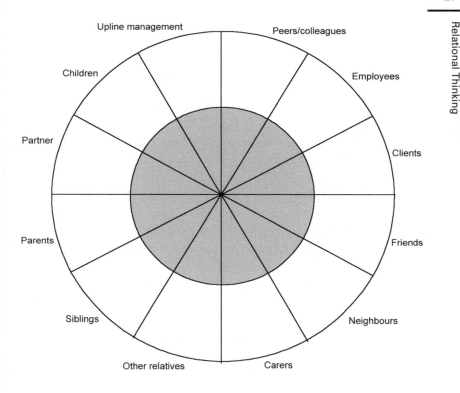

DIAGRAM 3: An unfilled relational base. The grey area shows your closest relationships.

◆ How big is the disparity between the company's highest and lowest earner?

◆ Do you have opportunities to meet partners and relatives of work colleagues – for instance, at office parties and outings?

◆ Are there any opportunities for job sharing?

◆ Do you and your colleagues experience home/work tensions? Does the company address this?

◆ What is the office layout? How are personnel allocated between different sites?

◆ Are offices open-plan or closed? What relational effects does this have?

3. Consider the value of treating relationships as ends, not just as means

This is a real issue in business, where there can be so much pressure from the bottom line.

Go to the arrivals area at any big airport and you will see – free of charge – a living demonstration of relationships treated as ends and not means. People greeting their loved ones are not thinking how the relationship is going to help them. They are not making calculations. The joy and the value is vested in the relationship itself.

At the other end of spectrum, visit the customer relations manager in a bank. It would be churlish to label every encounter with service personnel as insincere. After all, most of us would rather be smiled at than greeted with a surly scowl. Nevertheless, we are aware of another, largely economic agenda floating somewhere in the background. The bank has an interest in cultivating our goodwill.

Naturally enough, the cheerful and obliging manner will not survive a really serious challenge – such as the many bank clients who have lost their jobs and need to renegotiate the terms of their mortgages. It's here that a focus on good relationships really counts. In the long term, it's sincerity that builds genuine loyalty between the business and those who have dealings with it. And if employees are allowed to demonstrate that sincerity, they will have the satisfaction of knowing they have acted with integrity towards customers and suppliers.

Relational Proximity

As early as 1995, a report from a leading British think tank concluded, 'Many companies acknowledge that measures of the strength of the relationship are predictive of future financial performance.' It added, however, 'More work is needed to find robust measures for the full range of key relationships.'[1]

The mistake often made is to assume that strong relationships automatically exist in business – either because the top management says they do or just because people are working in the same building.

But strong relationships *don't* automatically exist. The structure that defines Kate as Derek's line manager doesn't in itself provide the trust and mutual understanding they need to make the connection work. In a busy office or, worse, if one of them is teleworking, forming any kind of meaningful relationship proves challenging.

This distinction between relationships 'on paper' and relationships 'in practice' is one we need to take seriously. It's the second, not the first, that fuels successful enterprise. How, though, do you make paper relationships work on the ground? Isn't it just a matter of whether two people happen to get along?

Well, no, it isn't. The various kinds of stress in relationships – based around differences of style and temperament, cultural divisions, professional jealousies, competition for resources or preferment, office politics or the importing of aggravations from outside the workplace – all diminish markedly in intensity if managers establish underlying conditions that allow relationships to build rather than deteriorate. Similarly, with such underlying conditions in place, positive outcomes – such as trust, cooperation, teamwork, morale – correspondingly strengthen.

The research on which this is based was first published in 1993 and has been road-tested in numerous organizations – including businesses, schools, hospitals and prisons – in the years since.[2]

It centres on just *five* qualities (shown in Diagram 4) – *encounter, storyline, knowledge, fairness* and *alignment* – which must be present in order for a relationship to thrive.

DIRECTNESS creates **ENCOUNTER**
CONTACT

CONTINUITY creates **STORYLINE**
TIME

MULTIPLEXITY creates **KNOWLEDGE**
INFORMATION

PARITY creates **FAIRNESS**
POWER

COMMONALITY creates **ALIGNMENT**
PURPOSE

DIAGRAM 4: Relational proximity in the five relationship domains

Encounter: How far do you practise directness of contact?

 Encounter can be symbolized by the image of an eye.

Email, BlackBerries, texting and videoconferencing are all fabulous assets. But direct, face-to-face communication remains the 'gold standard' for relating. So how far, and how often, do you and your team engage in direct interaction?

Important relationships, and important situations, stand in particular demand of directness – hence the finding by the Leadership Trust that more than half of managers find it more difficult to motivate and lead remote workers than other employees.[3] A staff grievance can't be solved by emailing from the other side of the world. As soon as possible, you need to sit across a table and look that person in the eye. Personal meetings increase your ability to pick up danger signals – you learn far more by reading faces than you do by reading voices or text. They also make other people feel you're accessible, especially if you don't use a Personal Assistant to keep people out.

Direct communication stimulates openness and disclosure, and gives people time to raise the kinds of questions and problems it's hard to air on the phone. That means fewer misunderstandings further down the road and less chance of junior staff being thrown in the deep end unprepared.

The sense of connecting, of experiencing the unmediated presence of another person, is both a deep human need and a vital support for effective communication. In reality, the number of people you can relate to directly will be limited, resulting in trade-offs and the opportunity for using a skilful combination of direct interaction and technology.

Storyline: How strong is the continuity of relationship over time?

Storyline is something that builds on a timeline: hence the symbol of the clock.

When the Relationships Foundation carried out an audit for a leading law firm, they found that pressure of work was causing non-partners to leave the firm early in their careers, driving a high staff turnover. The firm had set up its relational structure in such a way as to diminish morale and reduce its ability to attract and retain top quality talent. Financially, they were incurring high additional costs for recruitment and induction to replace staff who left.[4] Two-thirds of the partners and non-partners interviewed said there simply wasn't enough time to build relationships.

A certain amount of personnel change is invigorating for an organization. But you only reap the benefits of trust and mutual understanding if relationships are allowed to settle and grow. In the USA, the average 32-year-old has worked for nine companies.[5] It's not surprising, perhaps, that only 53 per cent of American employees can say they trust the people they work with 'a lot'.[6]

If you're a manager, keeping regular contact with line staff helps you provide adequate monitoring and quality control. It keeps teamwork coordinated and focused. And it helps you manage change by encouraging good handovers at points of staff transition. Continuity matters too in relationships outside the organization. If you don't see customers often enough, you know less about them. As a result, you can't meet their needs with the required precision, and they don't feel cared for.

A strong relationship is one in which the participants can look back down the timeline and identify a shared story. That story in turn lends significance to present encounters and establishes expectations for the future. Such continuity brings significant benefits in terms of trust, understanding and a sense of belonging. The costs of discontinuity include increased risk, loss of essential knowledge and the necessity to reinvest time in building duplicate relationships.

Time can be considered as the currency of relationship. Strategies for building continuity include the allocation of time, recognition of the time costs imposed on others and the management of gaps between interactions. Continuity must always be able to embrace change, without which growth and development is impossible.

Knowledge: How deep is the information shared in your relationships?

 Knowing another person across different occasions and in different contexts gives relationships extra strength.

Continuity over time naturally tends to deepen relationships. It does this by building up multiplexity – layers of connection between two individuals that operate in different spheres but are nonetheless mutually reinforcing. Playing a round of golf, meeting families at a social evening, going on staff retreats – all these strategies build knowledge and strengthen multiplexity.

Knowledge often surprises. The person who looks after payroll turns out to spend his weekends mountaineering. The CFO gives donations to an orphanage in Namibia and travels there once a year to help out. On top of that, people behave differently outside the workplace. You see what other relationships they have, what drives them, how they deal with non-work situations. And the same the other way around.

This two-way added depth in itself tends to enhance trust and a sense of mutual accountability. It also gives you an insight into the pressures a colleague is under from directions other than work. You're better able to anticipate crises and able to give more effective support. Not least, seeing people 'out of context' may reveal skills and potentials you never knew they had.

Fairness: How serious is the emphasis on parity and mutual respect?

Parity creates balance of advantage.

Loss of respect and relational distance occur most easily where there are marked differences of status, ability, remuneration or recognition. Thus parity tends to be more of an issue *between* management levels than across them, and most scope for personal action lies in your relationships with those who report to you.[7]

Where parity exists, it establishes a rationale for engagement and investment in a relationship, reducing the likelihood of industrial action and tribunal claims.[8] Where it does not exist, and where risk and return are not equitably distributed in a relationship, the result is likely to be disengagement. As the British union leader Jack Jones put it on one occasion, 'There's never been a strike about pay, only about pay differentials.'

The grounds for respect have to be real. But there are many different scales on which status, power and influence can be measured – financial, political, intellectual, hierarchical and charismatic – and the perception of parity will involve some conscious and unconscious trade-offs between these different scales. Greg may have wider responsibilities than his PA Emily, but he relies heavily on her organizational abilities, which he knows he cannot match.

These trade-offs are facilitated and made explicit by workplace roles, which imply not one single pyramid of seniority but a number of broadly equivalent pyramids, each representing a different skill base. Thus, while you may not feel greatly impressed by your IT technician's prospects in management, you may well be in awe of the speed with which he puts your broken laptop back on the road.

Lack of mutual respect can cause systemic as well as interpersonal problems. A friend, who is one of the UK's top scientists and a Fellow of the Royal Society, observed after a visit to Japan that research progress there was severely hampered by the fact that students must always defer to the opinions of the professor, even if he or she is clearly in error.

At the same time, though, parity does not require you to do away with accountability and reporting structures. The same scientist also complained that he'd asked a colleague in Cambridge to remove a piece of equipment from the lab and had been met with a blunt refusal. In other words, while too little parity in the company structure stifles dissent and innovation, too much of it can result in time-wasting negotiations over trivia.

Not all parity issues are structural. You can encourage or reduce parity simply by your management style. One key question, for example, is how much participation in decision-making you encourage from those who work for you. Raising involvement can result in stronger morale and commitment and a flow of useful new ideas, with a consequent impact on quality of output and initiative in problem-solving. On the other side, if one person on your team thinks another person is getting preferential treatment, the result will be dissent, undermined morale and loss of motivation.

Alignment: How extensive is shared purpose and therefore shared identity?

All organizations are intricate mechanisms in which people work together towards shared goals.

This concept of *commonality* is fairly well understood at corporate level, though not always effectively applied. When the US software manufacturer Lotus added 'Have fun!' to its list of basic company values, Americans understood instinctively. However, workers at its Dutch operation found the invitation intrusive.[9] Cultural differences can divide us, even if we were raised in the same town. But building a sense of shared identity, and constructing a set of genuinely shared objectives, both enhances communication between company employees and drives productivity.

Where relationships in an organization are characterized by shared purpose, petty annoyances and interpersonal rivalries proportionately lose their influence. For many years now, exercises in corporate team-building have focused on precisely this area. But, of course, obtaining a fundamental buy-in from your staff and colleagues calls a lot of things into question, including just how compatible the corporate objectives are with the life goals of those on the corporation's payroll, and how quickly commitments to staff 'valued as members of our corporate family' are laid aside when the economic going gets tough.

The key concept: Relational proximity

Where these positive qualities of relationship exist – where there is encounter, shared storyline, mutual knowledge, a perception of fairness, and an alignment of purpose – there is a high chance of relationships working: relationships between colleagues, between management levels, between family members, between friends. In this book we summarize this state of relationships with a single expression: *relational proximity.*

In organizational terms, the benefits of relational proximity tend to play out as follows:

DIMENSION of relational proximity	FEATURE of relationship	EXPERIENCE in relationships	OUTCOME for organization
Greater...	creates...	encouraging...	and producing...
directness	encounter	connectedness	communication
continuity	storyline	belonging	momentum in relationship
multiplexity	knowledge	mutual understanding	transparency
parity	fairness	mutual respect	participation
commonality	alignment	shared identity	synergy

Relationships rarely break down where relational proximity is truly present. Almost always, discord indicates not an excess of relational proximity but that some aspect of it is weak or missing. Overstretched pay differentials will undermine fairness, replacing respect with criticism and weakening participation. A new appointment in a team will take time to settle in, precisely because they do not yet share the team's story and mutual knowledge. During this learning period, misunderstandings can occur and a team can suffer some loss of direction.

From a management perspective, the important point is this. In any relationship you participate in, the dimensions of *directness, continuity, multiplexity, parity* and *commonality* constitute five variables you can adjust in order to maximize the chances of the relationships strengthening. (These variables are shown in the first column of the table above. They also appear in Diagram 4 at the beginning of this chapter.) Exactly how you do this, across a wide range of areas and situations, is the subject matter of the rest of this book.

In the majority of businesses and public service organizations, levels of relational proximity are depleted. In effect, this means that various kinds of clutter have been allowed to get in among the individuals and stakeholder groups and to prevent relationships building. One massive problem with PLCs, for example, is simply that the owners of the business – the shareholders – have almost no meaningful contact with management or other employees.

Even within their own reporting structures, organizations are notoriously bad at clearing this clutter out. Most offices are driven by an endless stream of tasks and deadlines, and it's simply assumed that employees will have enough social skills to cooperate in getting the tasks done and the deadlines met. It's comparatively rare for an employer to step back and ask, 'How can we ensure that working relationships here boost our productivity?' or 'Are we paying enough attention to the relationships we rely on for our business?'

Ways to implement relational proximity

Typically, in modern organizations, the opportunity for relationship-building between individuals and stakeholder groups is at best constrained and at worst systematically choked off.

Job turnover and time crunches will restrict your ability to know well even other members of your immediate team. Further out in the company, your connection with others will likely be functional rather than personal. Little incentive will be provided to build relationships with outsiders such as buyers, sellers or service providers. The chances are you could pass a company board member on the street and not know it. And as for the vast crowd of people who actually own the company at any given moment through its shares, you won't have the faintest clue who they are.

The opportunities available to you to build relational proximity in your company are huge and different at every level. Some involve simple changes of habit or behaviour. Others are based in departmental or organizational policy and procedures. Still others call into question the way we structure whole companies and even the way we organize capitalization through the markets.

But, at every level, the first step is to take seriously the crucial role of relationships in making any kind of organization work. If there are no 'agents of change' in a company, nothing will happen. And to be an agent of change you really have to start by looking at your own relationships.

As a way to begin, take just one important one-to-one meeting you have scheduled in the next few days and examine your relationship with the other person using the concept of relational proximity. Here are some ideas to start with.

1. Use directness to promote encounter

Think forward to the meeting and make some resolutions about how you are going to handle it. Directness means practising total engagement with the person you are meeting. You want to get the most out of the meeting itself and at the same time keep the meeting as appropriately short as possible. Determine to listen, to focus on the conversation in the present, and to give the right feedback – through your facial expression and the way you use your voice – so the other person knows that you are

fully engaged. Take note in advance of the other matters that
will compete for your attention – the next meeting, the pressure
on your budget – and mentally park them for the time you are
in conversation.

2. Use continuity to build storyline
Before the meeting, orient yourself in the story of the relationship.
Every relationship has a story, whether it's a relationship with
a colleague, a customer, a supplier or with a friend or family
member. Take a few moments to think about the history of
the relationship and where you think it might go in the future.
Where have you met this person before? How often have you
met? What happened on the last occasion? Would you say
that the relationship is developing or declining, increasing or
decreasing in importance? Where would you like it to be in a
year's time, and how does the current business under discussion
bear on those long-term aims?

3. Use multiplexity to increase knowledge
Building multiplexity in a relationship often requires you to
explore life outside our shared past history. With a new contact,
you may find conversational leads in information available in
the bio on a company website or in an internal job description.
With people you already know, review what information has
already been shared in previous meetings – information you
may have lost sight of in the intervening period. Talk to mutual
acquaintances with a view to getting a broader understanding
of the person you are going to meet or a fresh angle on what
interests and motivates that person.

4. Use parity to encourage fairness
To what extent are you conscious of differences in rank? On
what are these differences based? And how does the difference
look when viewed from the other side of the relationship? The
person you're meeting may occupy a different level of seniority,
be better or less known, have a higher or lower income, have
a more assertive or more retiring personality, be more or less
talented, or even just have better or worse looks. Because

perceived disparity can impede relationships, it's important to avoid power plays with those who may feel disadvantaged next to you and to identify in yourself the sources of discomfort if you feel yourself the 'junior partner'. Remember that parity in one area can compensate for disparity in another and that a sense of parity is usually comfortable for both parties.

5. Use commonality to create alignment

In some ways, this is about looking for common ground, insofar as a shared interest tends to make people feel as if they are on the same footing. In organizational terms, ask what the other person's objectives are, and what are your own, both for the meeting itself and, in a wider context, for your role in the organization over the next year. What are the main factors driving these objectives? To what extent do your values and the other person's values correspond with one another? What are the points of variance? And what outcome to the meeting would represent a win–win situation for both of you, given the objectives described above?

Relational Time Management

Michael Askey was about to board a flight to Geneva when he realized he'd lost something important. He patted his pockets, turned out his hand luggage, patted his pockets again, then fought his way through to the steward at the boarding gate.

'Look, I think I left my phone at the security check. Do I have time to go back?'

She eyed the clock. 'The plane's leaving in twenty minutes.'

'I'll take the train back to the terminal.'

'You're not allowed to take the train back,' she said. 'The train only carries passengers one way. I can call the security check if you want.' She picked up the receiver on her desk.

Michael tapped his foot impatiently. How could he have lost a mobile phone? He'd arrived at the airport with the device jammed between his shoulder and his jaw, trying to squeeze in all those crucial calls before he left the country. He'd had it with him as he got his foreign currency and bought some last-minute insurance. Then he put it down to go through the security check – and just left it behind.

'What make is it?' asked the steward.

'A Motorola.'

'They have it. If you want, they can send it to Lost and Found.'

For a moment, his hopes rose. 'Where's that?'

'At the other end of the airport.'

Michael thanked her and went back to his seat, feeling dejected.

But at least the phone hadn't been stolen. Really, all he had to do was contact his secretary and arrange for it to be returned to his office before he got back. He still had fifteen minutes left before take-off. Instinctively, he reached into his pocket to make the call...

Packing the suitcases

This episode typifies the modern problem with time.

Time is a finite commodity. You have exactly twenty-four hours in a day. Not a second more, not a second less. So busy business people try to jam as much as they can into the 'time suitcase'. The big essential items go in first, then as many small things as you can stuff in around the edges. You feel good if you can zip it closed. The day has been well spent. Nothing left out, nothing wasted.

Traditionally, good time management will also involve delegation, which means you get to put some of your stuff in someone else's suitcase. This removes time-consuming tasks from your schedule but introduces a cost in terms of coordinating other people's efforts and leaving yourself dependent on their ability to deliver on the deadline.

Time is money. Your company pays you for your time. You parcel out your attention and ability and experience in units of time, and the amount of money the company pays you for each unit reflects, in some measure, the value you add to the company during that period. The longer you work, it is assumed, the more value you deliver.

This use of time as a measuring device for useful labour explains why factories clock workers in and out, and why those who are not bound by the clock often work over hours. The manager's self-imposed habit of packing his own time suitcase full (to boost promotion prospects or avoid redundancy) has in most industries spilled down the layers of seniority to create a long-hours culture in which presenteeism – being seen to be at one's desk for at least the requisite hours – has taken a powerful hold.

The over-related manager

The adoption of telecommunication in business, which has accelerated with the advent of mobile phones, messaging and email, has fundamentally changed the way managers operate.

One effect of these technologies has been to pull interested parties together as though they were all sitting in one very overcrowded room.

This can result in efficiencies.

David Beyrouth directs multimedia shows that involve coordinating the efforts of performers, lighting and sound engineers, tech crews and support staff in and around a ballroom where 700 guests will attend a dinner event. The only way he can get the set up and rehearsals pushed through on time, he says, is to be in constant radio contact via headset with other members of the team. Otherwise, he would spend half his time walking from one part of the room to another just to deliver instructions. But the medium imposes its own disciplines. The radio space is a virtual room shared by the entire crew – only one person can speak at a time, and leaving your mike on when you're talking 'off-air' prevents any other useful conversation taking place.

Almost everyone, and particularly everyone in business, over the last two decades will have felt the change in pace associated with the arrival of email and the mobile phone.

For one thing, bounce backs just happen faster. When most business interaction happened by mail, you could write a letter and not expect a reply for a week. Now an email comes back the same day, accelerating decision-making processes. It's not unusual for managers to have over 200 emails to read in the morning, even excluding junk mail and advertising.

Over the same period, statutory working hours have changed relatively little and most of us have homes full of convenient labour-saving devices. On that basis, life should be growing more leisurely.

But, thanks mainly to changes in communication technology, daily living inside and outside the workplace now requires us to manage many *more* relationships. In the couple of hours before Michael Askey lost his phone, he had made ten calls to different colleagues, changed money, bought insurance, checked his luggage in. And all he was doing was taking a week's holiday.

We all have a lot going on in our lives. We have friends, family, cars, homes, insurance, groceries, banks, investments, home improvements, electricity bills, weekend breaks, DVDs, income tax, clothes, ticket cancellations, schooling, health – and that's before we even get to work. All these interests connect us to different groups of people, requiring us to make visits, send letters, reach decisions, use the phone. And technology, which accelerates our ability to respond, also adds new layers of frustration, creating lengthy call centre queues and absurdities such as the phone bill a friend received, charging him £00.09 (that's 8p in calls and 1p tax) – for which he nonetheless had to write a cheque, address an envelope and find a stamp.[1]

It's the same at work.

Managers are clocking up many more travel miles in commuting and business trips. And the increasingly sophisticated handsets we carry with us put literally millions of people at our fingertips (and us at theirs) at very low cost. Colleagues, banks, customers, clients, service providers, accountants, internet sites – we are in a state of almost constant interaction with all of them. Nobody is more than a click or two away. And our inboxes pile up because it's just so easy to be copied in on other people's emails and so easy to refer back to base when we're in negotiations. We're so wired up that we have to make a conscious decision to switch off our ever-present virtual community when we go into a theatre.

The result? Well, you know that already. The time suitcase just isn't big enough. And, particularly if you have a family, the competing demands on your quantity-time turn you into an obsessive would-be super achiever who is in reality sleep-deprived, underperforming, stressed, irritable and burdened with guilt.

You – and probably all the people who work for you.

How to get the most out of a unit of time

Here is a sad but true story.

A married couple, both with high-paying jobs based in different parts of Europe, had so little time together that they resorted to having a baby by IVF. In other words, they calculated that the woman had more opportunity to get to a fertility clinic than to get into bed with her partner.

We are all used to considering whether we are 'giving enough time' to people. The assumption, in line with conventional time management, is that time can be spent in a way analogous to money, and that achieving certain goals (financial, relational or anything else) will carry a more-or-less definable time cost.

We are also familiar with the idea of quality time as opposed to quantity-time – by which we mean, usually, time free from distractions, doing something that both parties find useful and enjoyable. You have quality time with your children when you take a day trip to a museum; the quality goes down if one of the kids is on the phone all the time or the museum is so crowded that you spend most of the day queuing or fighting the crowds.

The idea of quality time, though, bears a little examination.

Time we devote to relationships varies in value depending on the degree of relational proximity – that is, on how far we can draw not just on recordable hours and minutes but on a shared story, undisturbed directness of encounter, a sense of parity and fairness, and shared purpose.

So the museum trip, even with the queues and crowds and resulting stress, will go a lot better if everyone is comfortable with one another (connectedness), if the destination has been chosen to accord with everyone's interests (mutual understanding), if nobody feels railroaded by anyone else's agenda (mutual respect) and if everyone has bought into the plan (shared purpose).

In the business context, the same applies. If you and I have a sixty-minute meeting to hammer out a sales strategy, it's not really the quantity of time that determines the outcome. It's the *depth* of time, measured in relational proximity:

◆ We will find the whole negotiation easier if we do it face to face than over the telephone (encounter).

◆ We will arrive in a much better frame of mind if we've already done a lot of business together (that is, if there is story in our relationship).

◆ We will enjoy heightened levels of trust if we have loyalties and mutual interests outside the workplace (knowledge).

◆ We will deal with the agenda much more efficiently if we engage as equals and one of us doesn't feel the other is forcing his own ideas and solutions (fairness based on parity).

◆ And we are much more likely to reach a satisfactory outcome if neither of us is smuggling in private and undisclosed goals (alignment of interests).

Pushing up levels of relational proximity in the workplace saves a lot of time because important discussions are less likely to be hedged around with position-establishing pleasantries and subtle meta-negotiations over who is really calling the shots. If you draw relational proximity into your time management, you will almost automatically have more information at your fingertips about your team members' interests, strengths and skills. You can cut to the chase more quickly and more effectively. You are better positioned to read the people around you and to know how to get the best out of them.

Also, maintaining mature relationships is considerably less time-consuming than making new ones. The 'learning curve' the new appointee confronts is 90 per cent relational – building the foundations of relational proximity and therefore of unforced cooperation and trust. That's why offices with high staff turnovers can turn into relational deserts.

Time and relational wealth

A lot of the relational manager's relationships will remain purely functional. And that is fine. A five-minute exchange with your phone banking operative will usually achieve your targets, even when that operative works out of India and you will never speak to them again . But ongoing relationship management needs time. You can't create relationships instantly any more than you can create an instant, well-matured claret.

This creates a tension because relational management places importance on relationship-building that often has more long-term than immediate value.

George White is senior partner in a London law firm. He faces precisely this problem.

> The real issue in the firm is that we need our partners and solicitors to visit clients. That's how we find out what the client's problems are. When we visit them, they're not paying for it, and it's on their turf and their terms. Lots of new work originates in this way. The problem is that the new work may not be in your area of law. The visiting commercial lawyer may find out that the client needs advice on property. But his remuneration is tied to profits in the commercial department, not the property department. As a result, partners and solicitors are reluctant to make these visits. It appears as a blob on their individual timesheets – time when they're not earning. But for the firm the visits are essential. So the individuals can't afford to go – and the firm can't afford that they do not go.

Relationships in and around a company constitute a store of wealth that drives the whole enterprise. It's a largely intangible asset that nonetheless makes a huge impact on performance, as well as on the quality of life of both managers and employees. But you can't ship in this kind of wealth in a single, massive capital transaction. It has to be built up slowly through the combined efforts of almost everyone, under the leadership of relational managers who see the overriding long-term value of the investment.

The same is broadly true of any organization, including the family – and don't forget that what goes on in a manager's life outside the workplace can make or break success inside it.

Children can come into families that are *relationally rich* or into families that are *relationally poor*. It has little, if anything, to do with their parents' position on the pay scale. Research shows that relational poverty, not just financial hardship, accounts for the children of divorced parents being at higher risk of mental illness, of showing aggressive or withdrawn behaviour, and of being more likely to underachieve academically and end up unemployed.[2] This doesn't mean all children of divorced parents suffer these consequences. But the nature of your past relationships does much to make you what you are today.[3]

Furthermore, relational wealth, not material wealth, plays the greatest part in producing personal happiness and support. When you want advice and encouragement, you look to your relationships. When you want a good time, you look to your relationships. Friends and loved ones are your main protection when you're ill, bereaved, unemployed or depressed. It's there you find respect, love and commitment. By contrast, poverty in relationships – social isolation, lack of social skills, relationships crashing – severely reduces your quality of life, increases your susceptibility to illness and can shatter your performance at work.

How relationally rich is your company and your department? How do your company's work practices affect your relational wealth and that of your peers and team members?

Anyone who has spent time in central Africa will notice that – notwithstanding crises of poverty, war and famine – ordinary people in that region are often far more cheerful than ordinary people in the UK and the USA. Childbirth and bereavement have the same emotional impact everywhere. But the inherited relational wealth in most African countries is far greater than in the West. If there were such an index as GRP – Gross Relational Product – it's sobering to think that the UK and the USA would probably rank among the world's poorest nations.

The American social scientist Robert Putnam put the point well with reference to the United States, writing in *Le Monde* in 2000:

The problem is that Americans are so hard working they no longer have free time in which to see one another. The amount of time friends spend at each other's houses has dropped 35 per cent since the Seventies while, at home, families are a third less likely to eat together. There is also far less participation in civic affairs: over the past 30 years, the time Americans devote to supporting a political party has halved... In terms of social capital, America has become truly impoverished.[4]

Relationship investment in the workplace

Today, it can be argued, the workplace has become 'newly hospitable to sociability' in the sense that long working hours make it an important arena for friendship.[5] The people we work with and the people we know outside the workplace can both provide us with crucial social support. Work is as much a 'people' or 'relationship' environment as the rest of life is. It's just a different set of relationships.

These relationship networks can extend a long way – even including the staff in the bistro where you buy your lunch. The company is a network of relationship in which every employee and associate is a focal point. Everyone who affects the organization, or is affected by it, in some sense belongs.

These relationships can be positive and supportive, even when you're under pressure. Stay late to conclude that all-important deal, for example, and everyone will thank you. The boss's figures look better; the directors can turn in a glowing quarterly report; shareholders get dividends; customers get faster service and perhaps lower prices. You get approval and a sense of achievement, and your boosted confidence feeds back further into the general creative synergy. But stay late in the office every day and you are likely to do irreparable damage to relationships outside the office, relationships you will need long after you have left the company where you work now.

Getting workplace relationships right is a priority some employers take seriously.

William Sieghart is proprietor of London-based Forward Publishing. 'My philosophy,' he told the *Financial Times*, 'is about enabling people to do brilliant work. If I can get the atmosphere and the support right, they'll do that.'

The support includes free monthly massage, yoga classes and an obligatory three-month sabbatical every six years. How much time his people spend at work isn't the major issue. 'We all know,' says Sieghart, 'that you can get more work done in four days than five if you put your mind to it.'[6]

By the same token, distant or unformed relationships can carry high costs. You don't need much savvy to see that bad relationships in any organization spell inefficiency and performance decline, as well as a lot of stress for those involved. Not surprisingly, as early as 1992, management guru Tom Peters concluded that 'Today's wisest firms... are those that are tops at consciously investing in relationships'.[7]

Ways to implement relational time management

According to survey by the Chartered Institute of Personnel and Development in the UK, 'Two-fifths [of respondents] report that working long hours has resulted in arguments with their spouse or partner... Nearly a third admit that work-related tiredness is causing their sex life to suffer, and 42 per cent say that friendships have been damaged.'[8]

This is not the place to discuss the work–life balance, which has a chapter of its own. However, note that relational time management has to address time at work and time at home as a single integrated issue and not as two competing domains. The real issue isn't stopping work taking over your life. Nor is it the choice between earning money at work and having relationships at home. It's managing the whole range of your relationships – in work and outside work – in a way that maximizes relational outcomes.

The relational manager, then, looks for ways of thinking about time that provide clearer priorities and greater efficiency in the zero-sum game of using the day well. One of the purposes of mapping out your relational base, as suggested in Chapter 2, is to decide where to place most emphasis, and this must include our central, supportive relationships – ones with friends and family that often lie outside the workplace and which can't be maintained adequately by the occasional hurried phone call or email.

1. Do a schedule diagnosis
Use of time, like use of money, can be very revealing. So use it for diagnosis.

Look at your diary for the last few weeks and months, and then go a little wider. What actually did you spend your time on? If you drew up a league table of your activities, which – apart from sleep – would occupy the first three places?

More specifically, who are you talking to? How does your work day break down when you analyze it in terms of time spent interacting? Who did you spend time with, for what purposes, using what media? Did you spend more time on email or phone or in face-to-face meetings?

How you divide up your time will tell you something about your real priorities. You may well find you're doing something different from what you *think* you're doing.

2. Send your people home on time
The director of a leading UK think tank had one manager who, unlike many of his colleagues, always left the office at precisely five o'clock. Day in, day out, he was out of the door at five. At first the director took this to indicate a lack of commitment. But he soon realized that, although the manager kept strictly to hours, between 9 a.m. and 5 p.m. he got more done than anyone else. He would keep conversation short. He was focused and effective. He gave 150 per cent. It never crossed the director's mind to criticize him for sticking to the letter of his contract, and in the end he was sorry when the manager in question moved on to a senior position in government.

This story illustrates well the benefits of a focus on productivity. That focus, in effect, strengthened the parity and therefore the respect between director and manager. Making maximum use of available work time not only impresses; it also permits more effective time control, preventing work from spilling over into time earmarked for other purposes.

According to the *Financial Times,* half of middle managers say that long hours are caused more by inefficiency than by workload. Most would prefer to work longer days in a four-day week.[9] The reasons for inefficiency are complex. In part, they have to do with the ability of managers further up the line to set achievable targets and provide adequate oversight and support. In part, they relate to a loss of inner motivation and drive, which probably further reflects a decline of shared purpose between company and employee. Behaviours that are not uncommon in Western offices – inappropriate attitude, unreliability, reluctance to respect codes of conduct and making private use of the firm's phone and resources – are, in effect, symptoms of relationship breakdown with managers.

One of the key things you can do as the relational manager, therefore, is to impress on your team that you *don't* want to see them in the office after 5 p.m., and at the same time you want them to be very clear and fully supportive on goals, targets and requirements during the work day.

3. Measure relational opportunity cost

At last count, secondary schools in the UK had to meet 207 different government targets.

Who is responsible for collecting the information? In many cases, teachers. If we ask what is the opportunity cost of the teachers' time, the economist will tell us to multiply the number of hours used by the average wage per hour. That is what it costs, in pounds sterling, to obtain the data.

But if time is the currency of relationship, why should we not estimate the *relational* opportunity cost of the regulation? After all, the information gathered is not a 'free good' in relational terms.

The time that teachers devote to feeding data to the regulators has to be taken from other places. From time with their partners and families. From a visit they might otherwise have made to the pub with other teachers. From seeing parents after school. And, most prominently, from their concentration on the pupils for whose sake, presumably, the regulations have first been imposed. Furthermore, by calling teachers away from relationship time, the regulation process chokes off one of the most valuable sources of the knowledge schools seek to implant, because knowledge flows along relationship channels.

Asked what senior managers and executives really do, one of them replied, 'Talk.' He was perfectly serious. It's an acknowledgment that managing is, or should be, primarily relational. How the CEO and senior managers of a corporation divide their time is a crucial strategic issue because their time is the scarcest commodity of all. It's far scarcer than money, which is why large companies will often buy or lease corporate jets for their senior executives.

A useful question to ask, therefore, is 'What is the relational opportunity cost of my time today?' In other words, 'What relational opportunities am I going to miss by taking out two hours to do something else?'

And also: 'Who needs me to spend time with him or her today in order to maximize benefit to the organization?' Note carefully that this last question is not the one most managers ask. All too often they frame it as 'Who do I need to spend time with today in order to fulfil my agenda and my performance contract?' Which, of course, is a quite different thing.

4. Explore your limits

Even applying relational proximity to time, at the larger scale you still have to prioritize. There are just too many people in your spheres of interaction to form close personal relationships with everyone. So it's useful to keep in mind Diagram 5. It's a picture of prioritization, built on the fact that time is the currency of relationships, and total time available each day is fixed.

The area of the rectangle represents your input into your relationships and is the *same* in both cases. So you have a choice. You can concentrate on a few relationships in greater depth (a), or you can spread yourself over more relationships, which will push you in the direction of superficiality (b).

What you can't do is have both at the same time. So which relationships are most important?

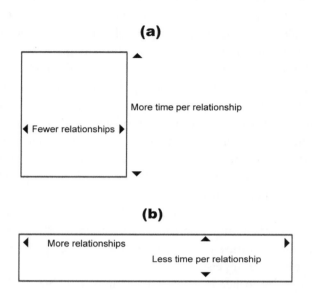

(a)

More time per relationship

◀ Fewer relationships ▶

(b)

◀ More relationships ▶

Less time per relationship

DIAGRAM 5: The number/time trade-off in relationships

5. Buy a better coffee machine

You, your employees and your colleagues may have a good deal of your social life invested in the workplace. You may share projects, share recreational time at facilities – such as bars, clubs or gyms – that are close to the office, even go home to shared accommodation. In that case, a good deal of blurring happens around the work–life boundary, and even 'overworking' may be both exhilarating and socially rewarding.

The relational manager will seek to make use of the fact that much of the creative thought and many of the breakthroughs occur not when people are 'on task' around a conference table but when they are taking unstructured time off. Certain kinds of informality should therefore be built into the work structure. As Professor Clive Holtham of City University London admitted, 'People are saying to me that the most important technology for knowledge-sharing is the coffee machine.'[10]

Relational Conversation

Early in 2009, the social networking website Facebook amended its terms of service, deleting a provision that assured users that they could remove their content at any time.

The implication was that personal data, including images and videos, would not necessarily be deleted from Facebook's systems on the request of the person who put it there. This in turn implied that Facebook had, retroactively, asserted ownership of all data entered on the site.

'In reality,' said Facebook founder Mark Zuckerberg, 'we wouldn't share your information in a way you wouldn't want.'

But users – businesses as well as private individuals – clearly did not feel reassured and 75,000 of them had complained. And despite having provoked serious questions about data protection and user privacy, Zuckerberg still failed to back down, writing on his blog, 'We have decided to return to our previous terms of use while we resolve the issues that people have raised.'[1]

At the time of writing it is not yet clear whether Zuckerberg will finally back down or not.

For a company that, only a few days before, had celebrated its fifth anniversary by publishing stories about estranged family members being reconciled through its site, this seems a striking example of how *not* to handle customer relations. There appeared to be almost no understanding of the way Facebook users might feel about having their rights withdrawn until an avalanche of complaints arrived to make it clear. And little understanding afterwards that the relational quality called trust might be a make-or-break matter in keeping Facebook ahead of its competition.

The conversation gap

In broad terms, what we're seeing here is the effect of relational distance on conversation – or perhaps lack of conversation – between stakeholders, at a cost to mutual respect and procedural fairness. But even when the parties share the same office space, the quality of conversation can be poor.

Does this matter?

According to a 2004 study by Career Innovation, 'In a very real sense, a business is the sum of a thousand everyday conversations.'[2]

When the authors of the study set out to measure effective conversations about trust, performance and success at work, they made some surprising discoveries. The study used an international web-based survey focusing on high-flyers in six companies.

They found that managers were central in the conversation networks. Ten out of twelve respondents said that their managers were the people they talked to most frequently. Yet 40 per cent of these said they still had a topic they would like to raise with the manager but were unable to do so. In other words, there exists a 'conversation gap'.

Among the explanations offered were these:

◆ 'Lack of quality time to have a face-to-face.' (25 per cent)

◆ 'My manager is extremely busy and worried with operational subjects.' (11 per cent)

◆ 'I have and am not getting what I consider to be a reasonable response.' (8 per cent)

◆ 'I don't feel it would make any difference as my manager has no impact on his upper leaders.' (5 per cent)

◆ 'I asked already but get no concrete answer.' (4 per cent)

◆ 'I don't trust him and I think he is not interested in that point.' (4 per cent)

◆ 'He is my new manager and so is settling into the position which may be affecting the way we work and how we work together.' (4 per cent)

◆ 'He doesn't solicit feedback and when I raise issues proactively he dismisses them or changes the subject.' (4 per cent)

These are not small issues. The study found that those with a topic to discuss with their manager were nearly three times as likely to be planning to leave their present employer, with lower levels of satisfaction and engagement. And this research, remember, was conducted among selected high performers.

On the positive side, good conversations made people feel motivated in their work (19 per cent), clearer about their work and career objectives (17 per cent), more self-aware (16 per cent) and generally reassured and valued (10 per cent).

The study highlighted the conclusion that many performance conversations are backward-looking – that is, focusing on records of achievement, often for the purpose of assessing performance-related pay. Conversations that guide the future of the business, of the team, of shared goals and development, are the ones being neglected.

About being there when you're not

On top of all this, workplaces have now been transformed by the appearance of advanced communications technology, which mediates important relationships and affects the type and degree of relational proximity achievable.

Since the landscape here is in constant flux, the key question for the relational manager is how new technologies can be used with advantage to improve – and avoid damaging – relationships, and specifically what they do to relational proximity.

Although electronic communication has quickly established itself as the norm, its impact in relational terms has probably been more profound than even that of the Industrial Revolution.

For most of human history, instant communication has largely depended on the receiver being able to see or hear the sender. You beat drums, rang bells, lit fires, sent smoke signals. Nothing more complex could be communicated without a person going along to carry or repeat the message. Hence the origins of the marathon in Pheidippides' legendary sprint to tell Athens that their army had trounced the Persians.

It wasn't until 1844, when Samuel Morse sent his groundbreaking four-word message from Baltimore to Washington,[3] that one person could talk to another *without actually being there.*

From where we are now, it's not hard to foresee how the various strands of modern telecommunications – mobile phone, email, instant messaging – will converge in a facility that lets us talk to pretty much anyone from pretty much anywhere at pretty much any time, with no regard at all for physical location.

Markets for fast, mobile communication are driven in large part by a need among businesses for efficiency and speed and by the pervasive desire for competitive edge. Naturally, the social consequences have not been thought out in advance, and only belatedly have regulators, for example, sought to legislate on mobile phone use – the fine in the UK for using a mobile phone while driving being introduced only at the end of 2003.

Meanwhile, being on the end of your own personal phone 24/7 has transformed the way people relate to each other both inside and outside the workplace.

Right at the start of the digital revolution, Dr Jan English-Lueck, Professor of Anthropology at San José State University, began an ongoing anthropological study of the world of professional high-tech called the Silicon Valley Cultures Project.

Silicon Valley stands – more than any other place – at the leading edge of our dealings with communications technology, and Dr English-Lueck's interest is precisely in what this technology, so readily adopted in California, is doing to everyday life. She paints this picture of a typical administrative assistant:

Sharon checks her email and voicemail in the predawn hours before her children wake to prepare for any tasks that may need to be addressed immediately. She carries a pager and a mobile phone so that she can stay in contact with her teenage children after they come home from school. All of them feel much safer for the presence of these devices. They can now stay out longer and be more independent since they are 'in contact'. The only time they have been physically together in several weeks is for the anthropologist's visit to their home for an interview.

One clear relational impact has been to increase the amount of time individuals spend on their own activities and pursuits. Since they can so easily 'touch base' with one another by phone, they feel less need to be in one place together at one time.

Linked to this is another trend: the growing speed and fluidity of social arrangements between colleagues, friends and household members. This correlates closely with the time management issues covered in the last chapter. Via the new technology, time is micromanaged in an exercise of precise and perpetual long-distance teamwork. As English-Lueck puts it:

Pagers, cell phones and answering machines are used in tandem to coordinate complex schedules. Work, school and recreational activities demand transportation, sequencing and division of labor... The perceived safety net of technology also allows planning to become ever more 'just-in-time'. Message machines and pagers allow plans to be created, shifted and coordinated in the space of a single afternoon.[3]

This fast-track activity depends on the lines of communication remaining open, and, not surprisingly, tempers can fray when someone drops the ball. Thus, one female partner explains, 'I get stressed when David doesn't have his phone on. You know, we have them for a reason, and I'll be trying to call him and I found out that he has the damn thing turned off.'

Your power of choice

Rather against the odds, the world has preserved for us a yardstick by which to assess the relational impact and value of current technologies.

Ten years ago, the author Howard Rheingold recently went to visit the Amish community of Pennsylvania, USA. The Amish originally came to North America in 1710. Three hundred years later, their way of life has changed little. Most still wear traditional, homespun clothes, shun the national grid and ride around in a horse and buggy.

To Rheingold, a self-confessed technophile, a trip to Amish country was surely going to feel like a visit to the Dark Ages. But what he found surprised him. In fact, the Amish *did* use new technologies – but only to the extent that those technologies advanced the goals of the community. When Rheingold tried to call an Amish contact, for example, he found he could only leave a phone message asking to be called back.

> I left a message on his phone, which I later learned was located in a shanty in his neighbour's pasture. I couldn't help thinking it was awfully complicated to have a phone you used only for calling back – from a booth in a meadow. Why not make life easier and just put one in the house? 'What would that do?' another Amish man asked me. 'We don't want to be the kind of people who will interrupt a conversation at home to answer a telephone. It's not just how you use the technology that concerns us. We're also concerned about what kind of person you become when you use it.'[4]

On this basis, the Amish have adopted a collection of modern consumer technologies ranging from disposable nappies to in-line skates and gas barbecue grills. This is not, as might appear, a gradual caving in to the realities of twenty-first-century living. Rheingold concludes:

Far from knee-jerk technophobes, these are very adaptive techno-selectives... the Amish have an elaborate system by which they evaluate the tools they use; their tentative, at times reluctant use of technology is more complex than a simple rejection or a whole-hearted embrace. What if modern Americans could agree upon criteria for acceptance, as the Amish have? Might we find better ways to wield technological power, other than simply unleashing it and seeing what happens? What can we learn from a culture that habitually negotiates the rules for new tools?

In fact, negotiating rules on technology is something Western societies do all the time. Just look at recent debates over genetic engineering or the sometimes fiercely contested laws limiting the use of firearms.

In contrast, for the most part we feel that technologies extending and broadening communication must be, almost inherently, good. They let us communicate more quickly, more conveniently and at lower cost. And thus our decisions to purchase this or that mobile phone or software package come down mainly to things like price, capability, ease of use and perhaps value as a fashion accessory.

But when you start looking at the world relationally, common assumptions are not a given. We should take evaluation seriously because quality of relationships is too crucial a factor in an enterprise to put at risk. There are many areas of commerce where the mantra 'unleash it and see what happens' would be simply unthinkable. And the comment quoted by Howard Rheingold – *We don't want to be the kind of people who will interrupt a conversation at home to answer a telephone* – is one the relational manager will pause to reflect on.

Moving office

Against all that, we have the elegance, the sleek beauty and sheer unparalleled utility of the mobile phone.

The great advantage of the mobile (leaving aside the add-ons of internet access, photography and gaming) is being reachable – at least in theory – everywhere and all of the time. As a time management tool, therefore, it is second to none. If you're going to be late for an appointment, you can call ahead and save the person you're meeting a valuable thirty minutes. If your teenage daughter gets stranded at two o'clock in the morning, she can call and ask you for a lift. And if you're waiting at a station with nothing to do, then, armed with a mobile, you can make those personal calls to family that otherwise would have dropped off the end of your daily to-do list.

But, of course, this versatility is, by the same token, the mobile's *dis*advantage. Unless you take a positive decision to divert calls, conversations with important people are apt to be interrupted by less important people who want two minutes of your time. For some reason – perhaps the fear of stacking up too many voicemail messages, perhaps the ego thrill of feeling significant – we feel under pressure to stay reachable.

There is also the matter of interaction quality. Mobile conversations tend to be brief, disjointed and fragmented. They suit coordinating and information-gathering exchanges. But hurried, on-the-move chat is less useful for sorting out personal issues or discussing things that require sustained listening and concentration. They increase connectedness – but they limit connectedness.

Often, it's the people at the centre of the telecommunications storm who take its effects most seriously. According to the *New York Times*, 'Microsoft researcher Linda Stone warned that we now live in an age of "continuous partial attention". Cell phones and bleepers mean that we are permanently available, but in a state of constant distraction.'[5]

So, issues arise over how much time in a relationship we devote to mobile interaction and how much we reserve for non-task-oriented, less interruptible face-to-face relating. What you do affects what you are, and again that observation from Rheingold's Amish friend demands attention: *We don't want to be the kind of people who...*

But as managers and corporate leaders, what kind of people do we want and need to be?

No email on Wednesdays

Shortly after taking over as chairman of the UK's Essex Police, Chief Constable Roger Baker posted a notice on the force's intranet. It said that, until further notice, on Wednesdays emails should only be used where 'urgent or strictly necessary'. Many emails, he said, were simply not necessary. Instead, his staff should pick up the phone or walk along the corridors and communicate face to face. Most business, he said, could be 'better actioned either face to face or with a phone call'. [6]

There are many reasons why email has taken over large areas of business communication. It arrives fast, unlike an envelope that has to be physically transported to its destination. And it is automatically and electrically logged and stored, eliminating the need for separate record-keeping or paper-copying. The minimization of effort involved in writing an email makes it a convenient substitute for writing letters and far more likely to get done when the pressure is on.

But experience suggests that, in relational terms, we have still not fully adapted to the medium.

At W. L. Gore, manufacturer of Gore-Tex®, emails and even phone conversations are discouraged. Instead, face-to-face meetings are preferred, as interaction among divisions is deemed crucial to the company's sales philosophy. The founder Bill Gore believed that direct contact was vital. [7]

For the twelfth consecutive year, Gore earned a position on *Fortune*'s annual list of the *US 100 Best Companies to Work For* and was ranked fifteenth overall in the latest rankings published in January 2009. [8]

Like letter-writing, email has to work at a distance from the receiver, without subliminal communication through facial expression or tone of voice. Unlike letter-writing, however, it does not have a centuries-old etiquette enabling us to interpret mood, tone and intent. The average email is short (making it liable to be abrupt). It is instantly answerable (meaning we're more likely to dash off a reply without thinking what we're saying). And it has not inherited from letter-writing the formalities of politeness (meaning we may fail to signal due respect for the recipient). [9]

In business, much attention has been paid to flaming – the predominantly male practice of sending abusive or insulting email messages. Email's screen-to-screen directness and lack of face-to-face contact make it easy to abuse. Even well-intentioned criticism can seem bracingly blunt. And the speed of the system causes retaliation to escalate fast. A 2003 report cited by management-issues.com revealed that out of a poll of 3,400 workers, one in six said they had been bullied by email, with 3 per cent claiming they had quit rather than face more of it.[10]

But the presence of email – as well as the sheer volume of communication it generates – is changing the relational environment of offices in more fundamental ways.

The ease with which information can be copied and sent leads to email overload – people receiving material they don't need but still have to process through their inbox. The effect is only made worse by email's ability to zip across departmental and international boundaries.

If you receive 200 emails a day as a manager, at an average sixty seconds each to read and reply, it will take over three hours to deal with them. In some cases, time pressure may be so intense that email replaces personal meeting even in the same office. A friend working for a leading financial services company says that, to save time and physical effort, he would often email his secretary, even though she worked just outside his door. To compensate for this lack of personal contact, he forces himself to walk round once every day to meet his team face to face.

Speed can also slow you down. Send a swift and poorly thought-out email and you will start a ping-pong game of requests for clarification. This could be avoided with a phone call. But in a busy office, replying to an email can end up substituting for dealing with the issue. It's an example of 'not on my desk' syndrome, and the effect is that email volume – and stress – both go up. This may be why a 2002 study found that e-meetings decreased group effectiveness, requiring more time for task completion and delivering less satisfaction to participants than face-to-face groups did.[11]

Also frequently forgotten is that emails have persistent life. Deleted and saved emails on corporate backup systems are now being drawn into litigation. In the Microsoft trial in 2007, most of the 3,000 exhibits were emails. And much of the dirt dished out on President Clinton over the Monica Lewinski scandal was recovered from the hard disk of a home PC.

Meeting on the information highway

Your company already has a website. It, or one of its products, may have a page on Facebook. More than any other medium, the internet represents your interface with the world. People who have no idea where the corporate HQ is, and know nothing about the company, can find your web presence in a couple of clicks.

In contrast to other digital media, much communication on the internet is presentational and seems, at first, to be fairly one-sided. Nevertheless, relationally, it exerts a powerful influence by determining how certain groups of users spend their finite time and how they perceive the company.

For example, websites for public services may go to extraordinary lengths to prevent a user actually contacting someone in the organization. In France, a leading internet service provider's website has no email support line, instead deflecting technical inquiries to a pay-per-minute phone service. By contrast, the global online trading site Advanced Financial maintains prompt email and phone support for all subscribers. There may be good commercial reasons for filtering direct contact with customers on websites (as with customer support phone menus), but it carries a relational cost.

Not just Facebook but a host of social networking and other interest-based sites run chatrooms, messaging and instant messaging facilities that allow text-based, real-time conversation with anyone else logged on to the same virtual space. Alongside these, low-cost internet phone services such as Skype are expanding to include file exchange, video-calling and videoconferencing.

Clearly, the potential for networking over shared interests is huge, with the added advantage that relationships are opened and developed without the aid of visual identifiers such as age, race or even necessarily gender. Despite the shock-gap associated with finally meeting someone you've befriended online, some evidence suggests that such relationships can transition into the real world. A UK study from 2000 showed 60-70 per cent of net users claiming they had formed some kind of online relationship, a few of which developed into either marriage or cohabiting.[12]

Overall, though, evidence suggests that social use of the internet tends to multiply virtual relationships – that is, in effect, relationships that are particularly low on connectedness and ongoing story – making them compete for time against the user's existing relationships with colleagues, friends and family.

As early as 1998, an American study of 169 people in 73 households found that 'Greater use of the Internet was associated with declines in participants' communication with family members in the household, declines in the size of their social circle, and increases in their depression and loneliness'. The report concluded: 'Perhaps, by using the Internet, people are substituting poorer quality social relationships for better relationships, that is, substituting weak ties for strong ones.'[13]

This may or may not be a direct management issue. But private use of the internet on company time on company computers certainly is, as also is the protection of company systems from hacking and virus infection.

Ways to implement relational conversation

A 2009 study published in *CyberPsychology and Behaviour* shows how fast the technological impact on relationships is evolving. Romantic partners, the study suggests, are increasingly likely to enter a 'jealousy feedback loop' through surveillance of the other's facebook page, where the page owner's interactions with previous partners can be monitored.[14]

Times change. And business is on the receiving end of that as Generation Y moves up through the management ranks. Managers who may feel uncomfortable with changing digital

communication will progressively make way for managers who
were raised with that change and embrace it. But, either way,
the relational issues stay the same.

1. Embrace the technology and ask the tough questions

If there is a new way of interacting with others – a new gadget,
some new software – don't sit there baulking at the learning
curve; instead, be the first to pick the thing up and learn it. If
you don't, you'll reduce the parity between you and more tech-
savvy team members and thus the grounds for mutual respect;
it will also prevent you from making informed choices as a
manager.

When it comes to communication, those choices start from
the needs of the organization. Ask:

◆ What are my company and department needing to
   accomplish?

◆ What relationships are central to that enterprise?

◆ How can I best use the technology to make those
   relationships work?

Here's an example. An international leadership training group
needs media products to serve both the training process and
its fundraising bases in the United States and Pacific Rim. The
media team members work out of the USA, Europe and India.
Close liaison is required on an ever-changing roster of projects.
Their department head reviewed options and selected Skype
conferencing for a Monday meeting held at 9 a.m. Eastern
Standard Time. He can patch in every member for two hours
at minimal expense. If bandwidth problems interfere with call
quality, he reverts to the normal phone line, despite the higher
cost of the call.

For individual follow-up, again Skype is the default option.
He took the decision early on to ensure that everyone had
high-speed laptops with webcam, so that individual calls, and
eventually conference calls, could be video as well as audio. The

team long ago abandoned courier delivery of CDs in favour of high-speed file transfer over the internet. They use an instant messaging service to carry on strategic discussions through text. It has the effect of keeping communications tight and to the point, and is more immediate than email. If someone else's contribution is required, they can simply be called in on the message conversation.

Significantly, however, the department head believes that this system works so well mainly because all the relationships are grounded in periodic visits to the main office by members on other continents. He estimates that once a year for two weeks is enough to provide a 'proximity top-up', during which they can clear a lot strategic discussion and decision-making. Those two weeks include a lot more than work. It's part of the planning that team members share meals, meet families, go out to see movies together and spend time socializing in the bar.

2. Never lose the personal touch

It's perhaps the most obvious thing to say about relational management, but the pressure to get things done quickly can often make it hard to do.

In a personal conversation, the chairman of a leading FTSE-100 company confided that he never commits any really important communication to email. Instead, he sends a handwritten note by courier. At least twenty other executives at his level, he says, do exactly the same. It's more secure and it never gets lost amid the email 'noise'.

The really important conversations we have – with colleagues, partners, parents, children – are done in person. Communication devices can help, but there has to be a foundation.

That bottom line in interaction is face-to-face meeting. There is simply no more personal a way to engage with someone than to be in their actual presence. And that ultimate proximity carries all kinds of benefits that even the best technologies still cannot match.

It's only when you meet another person face to face that you benefit from the full repertoire of meeting. The human face is capable of producing more than 10,000 distinct expressions.

Such is the importance of direct eye contact that we spend up to 75 per cent of conversational time looking at the eyes of the person we're talking to. When we can't see the other person's face, we need them to speak up by about fifteen decibels to compensate.[15] The body language, the nuances, the reactions, the emphases, the subtle shifts in expression – all are lost unless you are physically in the same space.

3. Include the technology in setting your own relationship rules

A large part of this has to do with prioritization – not just in the workplace but across the whole breadth of your activities and concerns. Because you are one person, not two; if your work arrangements ignore, underplay or disrupt your home relationships, you can bet it will come back and bite you.

Go back to your relational base diagram and decide who your important people are. Don't hesitate to prioritize them over others. Think through over the long term, and in advance, how you are going to maximize your relational proximity to these people. Consider what you are trying to achieve with each one, and what that requires of you in terms of connectedness, time, knowledge, respect and shared purpose. Set goals and make commitments. Know what you will do and what you will not do. Know when you are going to turn the phone *off*.

If you cannot guarantee to be around at crucial times with the people who matter, use communications media to get as close to actual meeting as possible. Set up a video-call with your children. Send your partner flowers. Emulate one CEO in the United States who has identified the hundred key people he wants to keep in touch with and calls every one of them not less than once a month – just to see how they are, pass on a joke or tell them some interesting inside story.

Another aspect of this is protecting time off for your team members. A teamship rule agreed among some managers in a large FTSE-100 telecommunications company is that no email can be sent over the weekend. Members of the team can prepare emails over the weekend, but they can't send them except in an emergency. Emergencies would include, for example, getting information to someone who's taking a 6 a.m. flight on Monday and can't access email before they depart that morning.

4. Do relational planning for your team

How are email, messaging, internet and phone use reinforcing, or detracting from, your relational planning for those reporting to you? Who do they need to be close to in order to further the goals of the organization, and how can those links best be fostered?

Physical proximity will always be a preferred part of the mix. Without it, you can't pick up those vital downtime opportunities when much of the real thinking is done – over coffee, lingering in the corridor, around a table waiting for a meeting to begin. Where there is strong relational proximity and high levels of trust, you may find you can start to create synergies – for example, by letting some staff work certain days from home, reducing travel, easing costs and employing virtual conferencing.

The relational manager will also set the tone in the way that communication technologies are used. Pay attention to email. Often you can save both time and misunderstanding by phoning instead of emailing, by replying only if necessary, and by placing overall relationship management higher on your list of priorities.

You may want to look at how you handle apparently aggressive incoming mail. Do you shoot back from the hip, or complain about the sender to colleagues in the same room? Or do you give yourself some cool-down time and check what's behind the communication? Do you blind copy emails, and thus put the recipient under clandestine observation? Do you set an example in clear communication and in honesty and integrity in your use of media? How often do you just go round the office and chat, instead of firing off commands from behind a closed door?

The underlying strategy is always to build relational proximity, and where those you need to build and sustain relationships with are outside the office, communications media will be essential tools.

John Mason, responsible for his company's operations in the Far East, received an email from a subsidiary group based in Tokyo. It said:

In the past your colleagues have made great efforts for developing our work in Japan. We've really appreciated their support. But one thing I am concerned about is losing such people from the Japan field. Two of them are now gone, and we have to build up our relationship with you once more. As you know, it takes more time in Japan to build reliable relationships, and the work can be rather slow compared with other countries. Please be patient and allow somebody to cooperate with us for a longer period.

Relationally, it's a contrast to the approach taken by Facebook.

CHAPTER 5

Relational Finance

In March 2009, a sexual harassment case was brought before the Central London Employment Tribunal by Rosemarie Corscadden.

Corscadden claimed that Jerry Lees, her former boss at Cheuvreux, a European equity broker within the Credit Agricole group, had discriminated against her when she refused his sexual advances. Two other women, she believed, had agreed to have sex with Mr Lees and had been rewarded accordingly.

According to the Daily Telegraph:

In 2007, the second woman she suspected to have slept with Mr Lees received a bonus of £201,040 which made her 'almost ecstatic'. Miss Corscadden, who received a bonus of only £154,096 in 2007, said: 'This was despite the fact that I generated more net revenue than her that year.'[1]

Spike Milligan once quipped that while money doesn't buy you friends, it does get you 'a better class of enemy.'[2]

Partly because it can be counted, money is often taken as an indicator of parity, and marked differences in access to money or monetary reward are apt to arouse feelings of injustice, envy or contempt. One of the reasons we mind what we are paid is that the pay reflects the value placed on us. Corscadden contended, reasonably, that her compensation should reflect her usefulness to the company and not her willingness to provide the sexual services that she claimed Lees had demanded of her.

Money is a major relational issue in business. How much the company pays you says something about your value. Many feel themselves to be undervalued as evidenced by their salary. And it is a common complaint among the lower paid that those with larger compensation packages are in some way 'on the make' and paid in excess of their real value – an impression powerfully reinforced by revelations about bonus payments to the bankers whose actions contributed to the global recession that began in 2008.

But the same disparities are often found inside corporations. For example, once you factor in annual bonuses and share options, a Tesco checkout clerk earns less than 1 per cent of the Chief Executive's salary.[3] And this sets up a whole set of secondary barriers. They'll live in different areas. They'll send their children to different schools. They'll take holidays in different places. They will travel in different parts of the train or plane.

The company, of course, may see a talented CEO as worth paying for. It may well be worthwhile for Barclays to give their Chief Executive a salary of £10 million, because a really effective chief executive in a large company such as Barclays could increase corporate earnings by as much as £500 million.

Nevertheless, there is a relational cost that impacts on staff motivation and output. The larger the differential, the more likely it is that top managers will be seen as 'fat cats' who are motivated more by the prospect of personal gain than by any serious, long-term commitment to the company and its stakeholders. In that situation, personal empathy diminishes between those at the top and bottom of the pay scale, and the widening wealth differential too easily implies a distinction in worth or dignity. No wonder top managers can find it so hard to get alongside their workers.

Contrast that with the man who, until the mid 1990s, ran a large part of the Indian Railways, which is still the world's largest single employer. Offered a top position in an international non-profit organization, P. K. D. Lee refused to accept the offered compensation, pleading that it was far in excess of his needs. By corporate standards, the offer was modest, yet Lee decided to take less than 50 per cent of it.

The point is not that relational managers should ask to have their salaries slashed, but that how money is used, and seen to be used, can have a powerful impact on relationships and thus, indirectly, on the overall performance of the business.

Money as social glue

In the 1960s, Martin Schweitzer was running a family business in London. It came close to going under when an employee overtraded in one of the commodity markets. What saved the company was the willingness of one of Schweitzer's close friends to buy shares when the share value was practically zero. The investment kept the company in business and quickly put it on the road to a recovery that has lasted to the present day. It also cemented an already strong relationship between the investor and Schweitzer's family.

Money has this socially adhesive effect when it creates relational proximity. Joint reliance on the same source of wealth establishes parity between the individuals and tends to foster a sense of common purpose and a shared ongoing story. Families experience this. So do employees of a small enterprise. There is a feeling that everybody's contribution matters; that the success or failure of one person's efforts will have consequences for all. And connectedness of the enterprise – the fact that members normally work in close cooperation – will act as an incentive for everyone to pull their weight.

Teams and divisions in a larger company tend to be less relationally cohesive. Employees are less likely to feel that the welfare of the company as a whole depends on their own performance. If the company is prospering, there will often be less incentive to push hard, and if the company is struggling, employees may feel that nothing they do as individuals can realistically turn the situation around.

For the relational manager in a larger enterprise, then, a big area of concern will be structuring incentive packages in a way that keeps an effective balance between individual and collective gain.

The problem has been summed up neatly in the banking crisis that began in 2008, which has exposed an incentive system that motivated a certain class of banker to accumulate bonuses while offloading sometimes massive risk on to the bank (meaning principally the bank's depositors and shareholders) and, if the bank failed, on to the taxpayers who end up bailing the bank out.

Read this assessment by the Professor of Risk Engineering at New York University, Nassim Nicholas Taleb:

In fact, the incentive scheme commonly in place does the exact opposite of what an 'incentive' system should be about: it encourages a certain class of risk-hiding and deferred blow-up. It is the reason banks have never made money in the history of banking, losing the equivalent of all their past profits periodically – while bankers strike it rich. Furthermore, it is that incentive scheme that got us in the current mess.

Take two bankers. The first is conservative. He produces one annual dollar of sound returns, with no risk of blow-up. The second looks no less conservative, but makes $2 by making complicated transactions that make a steady income, but are bound to blow up on occasion, losing everything made and more. So while the first banker might end up out of business, under competitive strains, the second is going to do a lot better for himself. Why? Because banking is not about true risks but perceived volatility of returns: you earn a stream of steady bonuses for seven or eight years, then when the losses take place, you are not asked to disburse anything. You might even start again, after blaming a 'systemic crisis' or a 'black swan' for your losses. As you do not disgorge previous compensation, the incentive is to engage in trades that explode rarely, after a period of steady gains.[4]

According to Taleb, 'Robert Rubin, the former US Treasury secretary, earned close to $115m from Citigroup for taking risks that we are paying for. So far no attempt has been made to claw it back from him.' This, in Taleb's view, does not amount to 'rewarding talent'.

Contrast that with a 34-year-old manager in a large FTSE-100 telecommunications company, whose bonus is fixed in three categories: 70 per cent in terms of overall revenue against target, 20 per cent in terms of new orders against target, 10 per cent in terms of customer satisfaction. All of these implicitly depend on exercising relational skills and building financially productive connections.

In the global recession that began in 2008, we have seen clearly the connection between money and family relationships as the contraction of the economy leads to all-round financial stress. Actually, consumer debt has been an acute social problem in the UK and the USA for over twenty years.[5] As one respondent to a survey put it, 'You can't help falling out, not because you start disliking each other, but because things are on top of you. And then again your standards go down. You get angry with the kids. Then you can't afford to buy them all the things they need.'[6] Not surprisingly, more marriage break-ups are caused by arguments over money than by any other single factor.[7]

The relational manager, however, is interested in how you make the traffic flow in the other direction – configuring finance in a relationally productive way.

Ironically, in a culture in which so much financial responsibility has been individualized (where we talk about *my* bank account, *my* insurance policy, *my* pension and *my* tax return), this has a lot to do with spreading risk and reward across business teams. In this way, incentive is connected not just to individual performance but to the performance of the team collectively.

Capitalizing companies

This is not an area you will be much concerned with in middle management. But, for board-level managers and CEOs, it's worth reflecting on the relational form and impact of financing decisions.

Although taking on debt increases the funds available relatively easily and quickly, it has a serious downside in a period of recession. The biblical proverb says that the borrower is the slave of the lender, and recent experience shows how often this is true.

In 2008, Urals Energy set out on an ambitious programme of expansion, amassing a debt liability of $650 million to buy a 100 per cent interest in the massive Russian Dulisminskoye oil field and a 35.3 per cent interest in Taas-Yuriakh. Had the oil price stayed high, and had overall production levels been maintained, and had credit not tightened with the economic crisis, Urals would have been on its way to becoming a significant and stable oil producer. As things worked out, however, the company was unable to meet its debt obligations to the Russian state bank Sberbank, and ended up, a year later, having to relinquish its acquisitions, the share price having meanwhile collapsed from 200p to less than 5p on the London Stock Exchange.

That the share price took its first steep decline when the acquisitions were first announced says something about the relationship between the directors and the shareholders, and the nature of investment relationships in general in public limited companies. In this instance, as in many others, debt financing loaded most of the risk on to the borrower, underlining the relational distance between those who provide the capital and those who use it.

Equity finance, on the other hand, has the relational advantage of distributing risk evenly between capital provider and the company. But a relational approach to company finance would go further than this. After all, investors should be an important source of ideas and contacts and in general contribute to good corporate governance. Market requirements about the disclosure of price-sensitive information should not prevent the company taking advantage of this resource. Relational proximity in companies could be increased, for example, by encouraging quarterly meetings to supplement AGMs and by inviting some other company stakeholders to meet the shareholders. Strategies such as this have the potential to build transparency, cooperation and brand image, and to reduce conflicts arising from the perception that the company is simply using its stakeholder groups in the pursuit of profit and shareholder value.

How exactly this might work out depends on each specific company situation, but it is important to recognize how flows of money into and through the company can become dissociated from the relationships on which they depend.

Ways to implement relational finance

In general, productivity and sociability are mutually reinforcing. In almost any enterprise, good relationships benefit productivity, and productivity strengthens relationships.

Nearly all important relationships have a financial component. When we talk about dependants in a family, we mean, principally, financial dependants. Friends may not explicitly support each other with money, but sharing of resources, splitting the cost of a meal and buying gifts are financial elements that help bind the relationship.

In the workplace, managers and employees cooperate to steer successfully the large financial instrument that is the company they work for. And around and between individuals the world over, in today's global economy, world markets give us fine but tangible financial links to vast numbers of people we will never see.

For the relational manager, implementing relational finance offers opportunities to ensure that relationships and finance work synergistically.

1. Get staff to engage with budgets

If you are in middle management, your budget may be imposed on you. To the extent that you contribute to the budget round, however, and especially if setting a budget falls within your responsibilities, be aware of the relational implications.

The final budget tells you a lot about relationships among the budget team. It represents the organization or department putting its money where its mouth is; in other words, what actual priorities have emerged for actioning over the coming year.

Budget numbers can be bitterly fought over or they can be set almost arbitrarily. Either way, once the budget is set, someone is accountable for achieving it. So how the numbers fall determines the framework of future interactions in the team. It sets the sales targets and the expenditure limits. It determines how many people you will be employing, how busy they will be and the chances of them succeeding in their roles.

Set the sales target too high and you please investors – as long as the orders come in – but may put your sales people under unreasonable pressure. Set them too low and you may fail to stretch the team.

If there is some control over budgets, therefore, relational management will seek to involve team members as far as possible in setting the figures. Participation raises motivation. It also imposes a greater sense of collective responsibility.

Under the credit crunch, a Singapore-based charity engaged in successive rounds of cost reduction. No arbitrary numbers were imposed from the top. Instead, each department head was asked to engage in an exercise of zero-based budgeting, in which every item of expenditure had to be separately justified. Nothing was simply carried forward from the previous year as an ongoing expense. Department heads consulted leading team members, and substantial savings resulted because every member of the team had a say in, and a degree of control over, the reining in of costs.

2. Look for the benefits of relational proximity rather than short-term profit

What appears to be a financial indicator is often, in reality, a relational indicator.

If the head of the sales team is given a twelve-month target of increasing the number of units sold by 40 per cent, that increase has to be achieved either by the formation of new relationships with new customers or by a negotiation within existing sales relationships. If there is limited scope to drive the price down in order to attract interest, this usually means the sales rep visiting the client to see where interests coincide in a way that could lead to an increase in business.

For the same reason, the best and most reliable trade is returning trade – where you and the client already have a relationship. The fact of previous sales builds a degree of continuity into the relationship; personal interactions extend this further, taking the emphasis away from the immediate deal and putting it on to the long-term relationship.

Toyota is one of a number of companies that have cultivated

the long term. When it first entered the UK and started talking to suppliers, Toyota did not talk about prices at all at the first meeting. They simply had lunch and tried to evaluate whether the company they were talking to would work with them on a long-term basis and have the spirit of cooperation required to solve problems jointly. That took precedence over any prices offered at the time, no matter how competitive.

Mark Adams, Toyota Motor Europe's Senior General Manager for Purchasing, was asked recently what advice he would offer other senior procurement officers looking to build long-term supplier relationships. He replied:

> Take a genuine interest in the manufacturing side of the supplier's business. Take a long-term view in your discussions with suppliers. And treat the supplier as you would like them to treat you back. We should seek to earn the respect of suppliers and the reciprocated support that brings, rather than demanding it as a right of position.[8]

3. Incentivize relationship-building

Incentive schemes play a crucial role in motivation, but the relational manager will run them under some fairly stringent tests.

As shown by the example of bank bonuses referred to earlier, it's vital to get to grips with what exactly you are trying to reward. Short-term performance, which aims to land the bonus within a twelve-month time frame, may actually damage long-term prospects by disincentivizing reliability and the relationship-building on which continued business and profitability depend. So, a relational manager will not shy away from the difficult question of how you reward people for developing good relationships with clients that don't have an immediate payoff, and will push to develop clear criteria for pay differentials, bonus differentials and increment differentials.

One of the key issues here is parity. Being able to show the way in which differentials reflect the value placed on a person's contribution reduces the danger of disaffection resulting from real or perceived favouritism.

A key question to address is the balance between individual and group reward. If bonuses are individual, you are setting up competition between members of your team and encouraging them to grab the business for themselves. Consequently, there is a relational argument to say that bonuses should always be shared out, since this encourages people to work in harness. The danger is free-riding – one or more members of the team being rewarded for under performance by the productivity of their colleagues – which will raise a parity issue of a different kind.

John Herrick runs a small legal consultancy in Australia, specializing in environmental law and strategy for resource development. He solves the incentive problem by requiring that he and his partners bill 100 per cent of their time to their clients but then put 30 per cent of that income into a kitty which is divided equally at the end of the year. Whenever possible, all three partners together will visit a potential client, without knowing in advance which of them will benefit most from any forthcoming contract. According to Herrick, 'It has worked beautifully for thirteen years, without one argument.'

The three partners have also agreed to pay for fixed overheads – rent, professional indemnity insurance, staff salaries – on an equal basis and in advance. So they are earning money after costs have been paid, not in order to earn enough for costs to be covered.

In a large corporation, the incentive environment can be slightly different. For example, as a middle manager, you may feel you have little direct stake in the company even if you own some of its shares. You get paid a salary, but the success or failure of the company as a whole depends far more on the board of directors than it does on your individual performance. In principle, however, there is no reason why you cannot encourage team effort and minimize free-riding by giving incentives an individual and a shared component.

The other issue here is timescale. Reward short-term performance and you will, in proportion, tend to disincentivize behaviours that encourage long-term stability. Bonuses set on an annual basis, then, may be counterproductive. In one large

FTSE-100 telecommunications company, only a percentage of the bonus for new contracts is paid in the first year. The rest arrives two or three years later, as long as the contract is delivering long-term value.

Relational Office Culture

The Gallup Organization concluded in 1999, after an exhaustive analysis of management style, that:

> People leave managers, not companies. So much money has been thrown at the challenge of keeping good people – in the form of better pay, better perks, and better training – when, in the end, turnover is mostly a manager issue. If you have a turnover problem, look first to your managers.[1]

You don't have to go far to find illustrations.

A report on management style carried on the USA's National Public Radio in 2002 included this contribution from a technician in a medical laboratory. Originally, she says:

> The boss went around to every employee once a week to ask how things were going. At first I thought she was merely trying to be polite. Other techs, however, took her question seriously and would tell her of recent instrument problems. She would listen intently and ask them how they think the problem would best be solved. I realized, then, that she cared about what happened in her laboratory. She was also quick to praise her workers in front of others when they had done a particularly good job, and she thanked them publicly for working overtime. If a tech made an error, she would bring out her work log and ask the tech to 'help' her fix a problem – a problem that had the tech's initials by it. In other words, an error the tech had reported out.

The lab, however, was taken over by a larger company, and things began to change:

> The new manager, by contrast, seldom ventured out of her office. When she passed her employees in the hallway, she would often look away, even when her subordinates smiled and said 'hello'. When approached about instrument problems, she would become impatient. However, she was also quick to anger if she had not been informed of these problems. She never praised or thanked anyone for doing a job well or for working overtime. However, if a tech had been slow to report out a result or had apparently made an error, she would publicly chastise the tech. [2]

Most of the techs, she reported, quit within a month of the takeover – and some of them had been there ten years. The lab hadn't changed, nor had the work or the make-up of the team. The difference 'was largely one of management'.

Edgar Schein's classic study of organizational culture splits it into three layers: artefacts (what you see, hear and feel when you enter an office or use a product); espoused values (what an organization and its leadership say about themselves); and basic assumptions (norms and practices built up through actual experience in the workplace).[3]

Management style has a direct influence on all three layers, and the nature of this influence sets the tone for a workplace and builds or erodes morale. How managers exert this influence goes a long way to determining whether employees see them as a 'good boss' or a 'bad boss'.

But a relational approach to offices and office culture goes a lot further than not being the 'boss from hell'.

Beyond Thursday pizza

Jack is an international estate agent based in Boston, USA. He runs his business from a ground-floor suite of offices he's nicknamed the 'Bat Cave'. A former Yale footballer, he's always valued teamwork as an ingredient of business success. But as his own company expanded and diversified and took on more staff, he had to work out how to make the teamwork real:

'About ten years ago, I realized I wasn't seeing people as often as before,' Jack explained. 'I was running around and so was everybody else. We never got a chance to sit down and talk.' Jack worried about the impact of this disconnectedness of his business, in which sharing information is critical, so he started a Thursday ritual: a free pizza lunch in the office.

'I know this is not an advanced management technique,' Jack said. 'On Thursdays, we sit around the big table in my office and we talk. There is no agenda. The group averages about fifteen people and changes members every week, but there is a core of five or six who provide continuity. They meet even when I'm not there. We all look forward to it not as a business meeting, but as an opportunity for informal talk. People catch up with each other, they brainstorm, they bring up stuff that doesn't get discussed elsewhere. And it works.'[4]

Traditionally, in every culture and all over the world, eating and socializing are linked – and not just at lunch.

Families and friends have their food-focused get-togethers at Christmas and birthdays. Lovers share their candlelit dinner. Business colleagues go out to a restaurant to kick around ideas. Almost all of us meet friends for coffee or join our mates in the pub or the bar. Eating and drinking with others reinforces social bonds and strengthens relationships. More than that, in the rhythm of the work day it provides a counterweight to focusing attention on the task.

How relational managers organize downtime – lunches, coffee breaks, social time – is one of the most important things they do. Why? Because in the rhythm of the working day, downtime plays a vital part in relationship building.

The office as living room

Relationships in offices are influenced in subtle and not so subtle ways by the space they occupy. Managers may not have significant control over layout and furnishings, but some do, and one company that has taken physical office design very seriously is British Airways.

The new British Airways Headquarters was conceived in 1989 and finally opened nine years later. Most offices are put together, rather like Lego houses, out of the same kind of units: square spaces, straight corridors, reception areas, desks (usually with computers on), filing cabinets and so on. In many ways, these things constitute our culture's mental image of what an office is.

But at BA's Waterside headquarters, architect Niels Torp deliberately set out to shatter preconceptions. An architectural review published at its opening noted:

> ... once you're through the doors, you're in a strangely different world. A stream bubbles along the floor of granite setts. Street-like things such as lamp standards and trees are much in evidence. There are cafés, a little Waitrose food store, a newsagent, bank, a hairdresser, a library, art gallery and so on. In the middle it widens out into an arena-like town square (Torp wanted a tower here to act as the 'church', but the planners wouldn't allow it).[5]

In the same way that Starbucks pioneered a trend to redefine the coffee house as a kind of shared living room, Torp took the functions of the office and housed them in something resembling an open-plan village. In a wired age, he asserts, there is less need to tie people to 'street addresses' inside the building.

> It must still be a bit unnerving for the old-style BA managers to see their staff having what appears to be a permanent lunchbreak. Mobile phones and laptop computers are much in evidence at the various (non-alcoholic) watering-holes along the street. When you venture into the office wings (each gently themed, like the tailfin art, on a region of the world), they seem half deserted. No wonder: as soon as you downgrade the importance of the desk, people are going to go walkabout. BA's project director Chris Byron is however

sanguine about this. Out in the street, people meet each
other more, he reflects (we are talking in a café, naturally,
rather than his office, assuming he has one). People, you
can't help noticing, spend a lot of time asking other people
where a third person might be found.[6]

The reviewer concludes, rather acidly, 'This is not architecture, in the end. It is social engineering.' But the underlying logic is valid: there is something to be gained by arranging workplaces around relationships rather than arranging relationships around workplaces.

Boxed-off offices emphasize status. They also provide places of peace and quiet where you are not being disturbed by other people's phone calls. Open-plan design may facilitate interaction. It may also increase distraction and make it harder to find places in which to discuss confidential issues. The coffee house is an important counterpoint to a formalized office. But how much time do team members want to spend in this less structured environment? And what efficiencies – social and workflow related – do you lose by hot-desking?

'Talk spaces' can be as simple as the areas around the water cooler or coffee bar, or as fully fledged and sophisticated as specially built 'chill out' rooms. Proponents have argued that dedicated talk places have shown that the conversations employees have with one another are the way knowledge-workers discover what they know, share it with their colleagues and, in the process, create new knowledge for the organization.[7]

A further and very significant matter is simply size. If you are in middle management, you may see size as just a 'given'. But before expanding the size of your team, or supporting the proposal for a takeover bid of another company, consider carefully the relational implications of larger scale. As in a household, so in a team or a larger group, the number of relationships involved increases exponentially as you add another person.

Writing for the BBC recently, veteran commentator Katharine Whitehorn noted about the UK school system:

The whole argument about whether comprehensives are better, worse or the same as the old unfair 11-plus has left this out – that half the problems of vast comprehensives are nothing to do with mixed ability, but everything to do with sheer size.[8]

Large public schools are broken down into houses of a smaller size, with a housemaster and house tutor and maybe a matron, so there are always at least one or two people who know about every pupil. In a large comprehensive, on the other hand:

A head in charge of 1,500 pupils can't know more than a few of them, and the place takes an entirely different kind of control. Certainly there are some marvellous heads who do make brilliant schools even out of these huge comprehensives; but never enough, it's far harder. [9]

The size problem affects all kinds of organization, from schools and hospitals to corporations and armies, and frequently undermines efforts to achieve economies of size in social structures, be they psychiatric institutions, schools, housing estates or multinationals. There is a well-documented link between small team sizes and crucial relational qualities such as loyalty, motivation and trust. Hardly surprising: with eleven colleagues, you have high levels of relational proximity; with forty, generally you don't.

A teamwork of friends

The 1999 Gallup study mentioned above identified twelve questions as 'measuring the strength of a workplace'. According to report authors Buckingham and Coffman, these questions capture 'the most information and the most important information' about what correlates with four aggregate performance measures: customer satisfaction, profitability, productivity and turnover.[10]

The questions are:

89

Relational Office Culture

◆ Do I know what is expected of me at work?*

◆ Do I have the materials and equipment I need to do my work right?

◆ At work, do I have the opportunity to do what I do best every day?

◆ In the last seven days, have I received recognition or praise for good work?*

◆ Does my superior, or someone at work, seem to care about me as a person?*

◆ Is there someone at work who encourages my development?*

◆ At work, do my opinions seem to count?*

◆ Does the mission/purpose of my company make me feel like my work is important?

◆ Are my co-workers committed to doing quality work?*

◆ Do I have a best friend at work?*

◆ In the last six months, have I talked with someone about my progress?*

◆ This last year, have I had opportunities at work to learn and grow?

Eight of the twelve questions (asterisked) deal directly with quality of relationships – co-worker to co-workers and co-worker to manager – and reflect between them all five dimensions of relational proximity – connectedness, time, knowledge, respect and purpose.

The link between performance outcomes and 'having a best friend at work' should not surprise us. Alongside leisure activities, workplaces are often the richest source of friendship, furnishing common ground in the form of shared space, shared goals and shared gripes. Some recent changes in the Western workplace have encouraged this – notably the shift away from noisy machine-based manufacturing to service industry, office work and more relationship-intensive work practices. Not all the changes have benefited friendship. For example, teleworking can make forming and maintaining work friendships much more difficult.

Friendship between employees delivers benefits to the organization, partly because friendship is the basis of effective team-bonding. At root, feeling friendship simply means that you like them.

Not surprisingly, therefore, studies have shown that employees who establish close relationships in downtime – discussing non-work interests, playing games, teasing, telling jokes over coffee – will usually also be found cooperating over work and thus boosting productivity.[11]

A report by the Industrial Society in the UK advises: 'Employers should give their staff more room to enjoy their work. Instead of seeing sociability at work as the antithesis to efficiency and productivity, they should see it as crucial to the bottom line.' It goes on: 'Gossip is the cement which holds organizations together. Providing communal space such as coffee areas or lunchroom, allows employees to share information, knowledge and build relations that benefit both company and the employee.'[12]

Note that friendship requires certain preconditions – on the one hand, continuity, shared purpose and the parity that encourages mutual respect, and, on the other, simply a reciprocal enjoyment of the relationship. Where either of these weaken, the friendship process can lapse or go into reverse. Friendship is, in sociology-speak, very context-dependent – that is, it often rests on circumstances that bring people together and give them opportunities and motives to relate. If those circumstances change, through reorganization of the workforce or promotion or downsizing, there will be a knock-on effect for supportive relationships among team members.

The danger point

As a relational manager, you cannot make people into friends. But you can establish the grounds and the opportunity for the friendship process to do its work. A large part of this comes down to creating or preserving parity as a basis of mutual respect.

Being transparent in your dealings, and particularly paying attention to parity among members of your team, goes a long way towards heading off socially divisive developments like perceived favouritism, cliques and defensive loyalties.

More difficult to contain are the emotional attachments. Only a few companies have laid down rules against romances in the workplace, and without much success. Banning romance in the office is, as one commentator put it, 'like trying to ban Christmas'.

The reason isn't hard to find. Relationally, the workplace is usually geared to encourage emotional connection. According to Susan Heathfield, About.com's human resources guide and herself a management consultant:

> People who work together also live within a reasonable dating distance and share a location, so they see each other on a daily basis. Co-workers in similar jobs may also be approximately the same age and share similar interests, both inside and outside work... Traditional meeting places such as neighbourhood and family events, the pub and sports activities do not present the same pool of candidates as they did in earlier times. In contrast, the office provides a pre-selected pool of people who share at least one important interest. [13]

In the UK, roughly 20 per cent of employees have had some

romantic involvement with a colleague, and one in six have married, or are living with, a partner they used to work with or still do. The jury is still out on whether the work performance of dating couples accelerates or stumbles. Much more concern focuses on workplace dating that takes the form of extramarital affairs or temporary liaisons.

The tendency of such relationships to unravel messily in emotional damage, inability of the two individuals to work together and possible claims of sexual harassment were highlighted in the previous chapter. To that needs to be added the secondary impact on colleagues (obligation to take sides, implication by knowing some or all of what's going on) and, in many cases, families (where a deteriorating situation at home can more or less neutralize a person's effectiveness at work).

Not least, managers will often need to take into account how such a blow-up will be received by the organization's key supporters.

In the last week of November 2007, the American Red Cross announced the resignation of Mark Everson, following the allegation that he had been having an affair with a female subordinate. Everson, formerly the commissioner of the Internal Revenue Service, was the group's eighth chief executive in twelve years.

As Ruth McCambridge, editor-in-chief at *Nonprofit Quarterly*, commented:

> If this had been a single incident, I'm sure we could just chalk it up to a little personal failing. But it's not a single incident... The Red Cross has been really rocked by reputational and organizational difficulties. If I was to look at any nonprofit organization and I saw that they had had eight leaders in 12 years, I would know that there was a problem.[14]

Ways to implement relational office culture

Relational office culture covers a wide range of things, centred around the management and conduct of relationships among

colleagues. Overall, the relational manager aims to set a tone
colleagues. Overall, the relational manager aims to set a tone of full team cooperation and conviviality. But this sometimes needs some thinking through in advance.

1. Set the relational tone

Inevitably, managers set the tone of an office. Given that staff may, for reasons of uncertainty or insecurity, stay too long, make it your business to ensure that work isn't eating up their time to build important relationships at home. Don't interrupt the holidays of members of your team with phone calls and emails. Do everything you can to protect their holidays and ensure that staff take them. As mentioned earlier, try hard to get them out of the door on time, and if they do work late, ensure that they take time off in lieu. Above all, in view of the need to preserve respect through parity, be impartial and treat everyone the same.

Make your own conduct the standard in politeness, consideration, respecting team members' outside relationships, and in the resolution of disputes. Avoid infecting your team with your own frustrations about management overhead or company directors, no matter how strongly you may feel. What you say about others powerfully affects their relationships – including, crucially, their ability to win trust and confidence. Relationships are long-term assets, but they can be blown out of the water all too easily by uncontrolled gossip and backbiting.

Make ample use of relational events to bring the team together. Coffee breaks are important and so are welcoming and leaving parties. Encourage spouses, partners and children to visit the office from time to time. You might even consider forming a sports team. The UK Treasury has a cricket team that has included the Permanent Secretary.

If you are in a position to influence dress code in your organization, consider the relational angles. Informality is the norm in some industries (for example, among creatives in advertising). But those who transact company business with outsiders, or who are visible to outsiders, will need to be aware of the link between their dress style and company reputation. It remains the case that, at the top level, you communicate a lot by the kind of suit you wear and where you bought it.

2. Manage the relational proximity of the workplace

How much does interaction in your workplace maximize the possibilities of relational proximity?

The answer may not always be obvious. Job sharing, for example, sounds inherently relational. But one side effect of sharing your job is a reduction in the number of hours you spend in the workplace and therefore in the amount of contact time you have with your colleagues.

On the other hand, some very courageous moves may pay relational dividends. For example, in the 1990s the Scottish Prison Service instituted a number of changes to working practices. To underline the importance of relationships in the organization, they started rewarding prison officers who had face-to-face contact with prisoners more highly than technicians dealing with computers and gates. More radically, they changed the way prisoners took their meals. Instead of collecting their food and eating in their cells, prisoners now used a cafeteria and ate at the same tables as the officers.

3. Make friendship a work goal

Because life throws so many relationships at us – not all of them sought – we are forced to make decisions about whom we will befriend. This is connected to use of time and the rectangles in the diagram at the end of Chapter 3. You only have so much time, and this obliges you to make 'quantity versus depth' decisions about relationships. Normally, we don't put a lot of strategic thought into this. The people we get along with turn into our friends and get the lion's share of our time; those we don't get along with remain our acquaintances.

The relational manager, though, will take relationship planning seriously and will take trouble to build at least a degree of relational proximity with every member of this team. This does not depend on being 'compatible', and a relational manager should be able to relate with ease outside their comfort zone. Some of the greatest rewards of friendship derive from the ways in which you and your friends differ. In the long run, you are likely to learn more from and be more enriched by those whose outlook and experience may be vastly different from your own.

Can bosses and team members really be friends? Again, this depends a lot on the way you set the tone. Friends, the writer C. S. Lewis once said, 'meet like sovereign princes of independent states, abroad, on neutral ground, freed from their contexts'.[15] The notion underlying this is one of parity – of neither side feeling at a disadvantage. Differences in seniority can cause problems. For example, a respondent in a survey on friendship and work recalled the change that occurred when her friend at work gained promotion:

> I can't accept the fact that she's in a supervisory role... We've just been equal for so long... When I sit there and watch her sign my time sheet, I feel ill.[16]

But parity doesn't depend only on rank. One side can be wealthier than the other, or more intellectually gifted, or more able-bodied, or better looking, or just older and more experienced. On top of that, part of your management role is to identify strengths and skills in your team that you yourself do not possess, and this balance of complementary skills should provide sufficient grounds for mutual respect.

4. Make corporate hospitality work

Corporate hospitality is not, fundamentally, about trying to impress visiting executives by giving them a good time. Relaxing together will usually tend to 'warm people up', but that isn't the final goal. You are using corporate hospitality with the aim of building relationships at their various stages – wooing, initiating, developing, cementing, deepening or celebrating.

In relational terms, corporate hospitality works because it encourages face-to-face contact, opens up non-task-related time and promotes a more open agenda. These qualities help you in three ways.

First, you can gain a broader knowledge of the company or department you are dealing with. The informal meeting allows conversation to range over 'irrelevant' topics which may nevertheless reveal new areas of opportunity or correct flawed and potentially damaging assumptions.

Second, you get a broader knowledge of the individuals you are dealing with – their values, experience, skills and roles, as well as the pressures and constraints they work under. This allows you to identify potential contributions and initiatives that would not exist with a different set of people. And it gives you a fund of conversational openers to keep relationships 'on track' in future communication by email or phone.

Third, the face-to-face element will always provide the opportunity of building trust, understanding and personal commitment. You can show respect for, and interest in, the person you are dealing with.

In short, you can lay the foundation not just of a business relationship but of a real friendship.

Despite all this, much corporate hospitality is still planned on a formulaic basis – that is, without thinking through what might be achieved. Given the amount of time and money invested, this is surprising.

One thing to ask, then, is how the structuring of a hospitality event is likely to affect relational outcomes.

For example, is there the right balance between entertainment (the game, the theatre) and opportunities to relate one to one? Are you planning the important relating times at points where people will be fresh and rested? And are you showing hospitality to the right people? Customers, suppliers, strategic partners, investors and staff are all key to business success. If your business relationships are the source of your profitability, well thought-through corporate hospitality should be a vital part of your comprehensive strategy for maintaining those relationships.[17]

Hand over relationships, not just information

Employees may come and go, but the organization remains. So hand overs matter crucially in maintaining continuity – in a team, or between yourself as a manager and those you work with inside or outside the firm.

Hand overs should involve not just transfer of information in the form of office records and so on, but, wherever possible, a personal introduction by the existing member of staff to the new member of staff in regard to the contact being handed over. This is most obviously important in the case of clients or major donors to an NGO, but also applies wherever a relationship is significant for the performance of the enterprise.

CHAPTER 7

Relational Systems

Ed Burbank, one of the USA's leading neurologists, tells a revealing story about the hospital where he works.

A young man was referred from primary care (equivalent of the UK's general practice) with loss of feeling in both hands. The primary care doctors had asked about his job, and when he said he was a painter, they immediately assumed he was suffering from carpal tunnel syndrome, resulting from repetitive strain injury to his wrists.

Ed wasn't so sure. He took a history. It turned out the man worked in an auto body shop where he resprayed cars with silver paint. Ed asked if he wore the requisite breathing apparatus.

The man replied, 'No, it was too cumbersome. We just use the paper masks.'

'Do you protect your hands?'

'No. They get covered in paint every day.'

'And how do you clean them?'

The man shrugged. 'The boss tells us to dip our hands in a tub of industrial solvent.'

Not surprisingly, he'd traumatized the nerve endings, resulting in permanent loss of sensation.

Had Ed not taken the history, these facts would have remained hidden and the patient would have received the wrong treatment. Why hadn't primary care found this out? According to Ed, 'They're so busy down there they don't have time to do anything.'

In many hospitals, he adds, the requirements for patient throughput have risen from four per hour to five per hour and in some cases to six. Ostensibly, the object is greater efficiency.

The actual result, as Ed puts it, 'is cursory treatment – ordinary treatments for ordinary conditions. But as soon as something extraordinary turns up, you're in trouble.'

The car painter is currently suing his employer.

Are relationships properly defined?

All organizations adopt systems and processes in an effort to ensure that targets are met.

In doing so, they define relationships. That is, either directly or indirectly, they set parameters in the five relational domains (contact, time, power, purpose, information) that are supposed to provide an optimal trade off between speed and effectiveness. The only trouble is, financial pressure nearly always ends up pushing down relational proximity levels, usually by trying to cram too much into the available time, with the consequence that the relationship increasingly fails to produce the desired output. A hospital that processes five patients per hour can report 20 per cent greater clinical efficiency than the hospital than processes only four. But at which hospital would you rather be a patient?

Another example of this is the telephone helplines that companies typically set up to handle inquiries. Automated systems have the great advantage of being cheaper and of filtering out easily answered requests for information. But the sheer difficulty of finding a human being with whom to discuss your problem represents a low score in directness, and the experience of being strung along in a one-sided conversation, most of which you are not interested in, underlines the lack of parity. If your query doesn't fit one of the preset options, some queuing services will simply dump your call.

Relational proximity is a live issue to customers in situations like these. They are not *experiencing* what ought to be the results of relational proximity – namely, a feeling of connectedness, being understood, belonging and fairness that supports respect. And when they don't feel these things, they start to disengage.

Contrast with this the way General Samson Tucay runs his

'last ditch' reform programme for rogue cops in the Philippine police. At the Philippine National Police Values and Leadership School, which opened its doors at Subic Bay in 2004, he runs a tough regime:

> We isolate them. We take their cell phones, their guns, their watches, their insignia, and anything else that would link them to the outside world. They are not allowed to receive visitors. We wake them up at four in the morning and make them undergo vigorous physical exercise until 8.30 in the evening. Mealtimes are the only breaks.

In this way, he deliberately breaks unhelpful and distracting relationships from the past. But the remarkable thing about the programme is the way it uses high levels of relational proximity between the trainees and the staff. Says Tucay:

> They do not hear any shouts from us, they do not hear any invectives. They receive no punishments. Anything that we ask from them, we first do ourselves. We sleep in the same uncomfortable wooded beds that they sleep in. When they wake up at four, we are there at a quarter to four. We run the same distances, we eat the same food. We lead by example.[1]

Silos and matrices

More widely, there are relational questions about organizational design, at the macro and micro level.

The term 'silo' is now routinely used to describe vertical management systems where targets are passed down from the top and reporting goes up from the bottom. Problems with silos most often occur where several silos are operating in the same area and there is a lack of cross-connecting relationships between them. As a result, managements in the different silos set uncoordinated and sometimes conflicting targets.

Exactly this kind of problem was reported in 2009

within the UK's Mid Staffordshire National Health Service Foundation Trust.

Faced with a four-hour target for waiting time at Accident and Emergency departments, managers in the Trust came up with an innovative idea of using two clinical decision units (CDUs) to 'stop the clock'. Investigations revealed that when too many patients arrived at A & E, some were simply diverted to the CDU. Although CDU treatment decisions were supposed to be taken in under twenty-four hours, and despite the fact that patients diverted there had no dedicated nurse to care for them, some patients were found 'dumped' in the CDUs for three days or more.[2]

This kind of example illustrates well the verticality of the silo. Once set by central government, targets funnel down into their respective silos, making resolution of conflicts between silos much more difficult. Meanwhile, the patients, who are the intended beneficiaries of the service, bear the brunt of the inconvenience and risk.

The fact that a health care worker reporting to the BBC's *Panorama* in 2003, on a similar incident in another hospital, would only be interviewed anonymously shows how strong a grip the target-driven culture can take in public service organizations. Vertical relationships within the organization simply outrank the relationships that connect the organization to the public. And, unlike commercial companies, public services often lack the disciplines imposed by a competitive marketplace in which the client can simply go elsewhere.

In an effort to avoid such problems, some organizations have sought to replace the basically authoritarian up–down structure of silos with looser, cross-cutting systems of accountability. BG (formerly British Gas), for example, divides its operations geographically on the one hand and by functional competence on the other. Unilever does the same thing, using region and product.

This matrix model of management de-emphasizes demarcation, turf and identity. Managers no longer ask themselves 'Who am I?' but 'Who is *us*?' Almost inevitably, far greater reliance is placed on relational proximity, because the system only works if there is trust and understanding between key players. In fact, it would not be an exaggeration to say that relational proximity is the single most important ingredient in making matrix systems work. Given that precondition, you gain greater creativity and innovation and a generally more mobile and versatile organization.

The disadvantage of this matrix-style management is that it adds ambiguity, complexity and uncertainty. You need much greater relational skill to build relationships across boundaries and groups. Getting things done depends more on influence than on authority. And the larger the operation, the bigger the challenge and the more reluctance there will be to abandon vertical command chains.

In the 1990s, someone worked out that a single Birmingham housing estate was receiving a total of £110 million every year in government expenditure. Because the money was coming down through a collection of independent silos – housing, education, social services, health services – and also because each of these structures answered national targets set by central government, considerable amounts of money were being wasted through unnecessary overlap and misdirected spending. And yet it was impossible to find the mere £30,000 required to appoint a local manager who would oversee and coordinate the use of government funds.

In the UK, central government generally has been resistant to matrix-style management solutions. And there is some logic to this. Placing more control at local level can make deployment of resources more efficient. But it also makes it harder to apply meaningful national standards because local empowerment means little if it does not allow managers in one city to devise educational or health care programmes different from those being used in another city.

Whom can you trust?

A third important area of relational thinking on systems concerns the use and abuse of information.

The fact that information routinely involves *information technology* indicates the nature of the problem, both within organizations and between organizations and the outside world. It raises questions of personal safety, identify theft, crime, fraud and corporate and national security. And the science of information management on the world's interconnected computer systems is so arcane that even the experts seem pressed to keep up with the fast-moving trends.

In this complex information environment, the underlying issue is relational: in short, trust. In an interview in 2008, founder of the World Wide Web, Tim Berners-Lee, commented:

> Another challenge to the Web lies in the media interface with the human being. Issues of trust, security, privacy etc. are very human issues. Phishing relies on tricking human beings. To combat problems such as this, we need browsers and email clients that more transparently indicate who is sending messages or who is running a website. Traditional security involves making cryptographic, coding schemes which are more difficult to break. But the issue for the Web is one of trust management. It is about how to design a system so that the user can recognize when a Web site that claims to be their bank is not. There are ways to help the user to manage the trust on their system and we have been talking about these issues for years.[3]

Clearly, the anonymous environment of the internet lends itself to fraud. So information barriers have to exist globally to prevent sensitive information falling into the hands of criminals, potential aggressors or market rivals. But the expression 'trust management' could be applied equally well to problems of information inside organizations. In a company all of whose personnel are unified under the same mission statement, on what grounds is access restricted to areas of the file servers?

Organizations vary in their solutions to this. Some only protect personal HR information. Others rope off whole areas of information from everyone except those who need it for their work. From a relational standpoint, it's worth noting that security is in part a parity issue. Confidentiality creates an information inequality, which can easily lead to suspicion and mistrust.

Economic downturns tend to bring such matters to the fore. If top management discusses job cuts behind closed doors and then issues redundancies without giving a reason, morale will suffer. Maintaining relational proximity depends to some extent on a willingness to be honest about risks. On the one hand, a public company will not want to draw attention to financial problems or allow price-sensitive information to leak out. On the other hand, management cannot responsibly ask people to work harder without giving them honest grounds to hope their efforts will succeed. If managers come clean about cashflow and balance-sheet stress, the resulting sense of parity and shared purpose will often stiffen morale rather than dissipate it.

Ways to implement relational systems

Changes in technology require creative and adaptable systems planning.

In sectors with rapid technology change, companies already established in the field sometimes fail or collapse because they don't adequately drive forward new business. One explanation for this is generational. Senior managers who are familiar with the old business simply don't have enough time to evaluate new technically complex business propositions. The only way for them to succeed in managing change is therefore to trust younger people to run their own new business propositions and associated budgets. They find this difficult to do. They lack trust in younger recruits. It's an issue of relational proximity.

The result can be loss of coordination. A sector manager in a leading European telecoms company was given a budget of £1.5 million for innovation, spread over four quarters. At the end of first quarter of 2009, every other manager at his level had spent his entire year's budget, so he had part of his budget taken off him to allocate to the others!

How much influence you have over systems depends on how

high you are on the management ladder. Here are some of the

105

Relational Systems

ideas you can try.

1. Ruthlessly apply relational proximity to creative challenges

Your job as a manager is to involve people in conversations. You are a convenor, a resource allocator. That puts you at the centre of your department's creative processes. We often make the mistake of thinking about innovation and creativity as products of individual genius. They're not. Generally, innovation occurs as a consequence of brainstorming and facilitated conversations.

David Ogilvy said of his advertising agency, 'We prefer the discipline of knowledge to the anarchy of ignorance. We pursue knowledge the way a pig pursues truffles.'[4]

Truffles was later adopted as the name of Ogilvy's influential companywide intranet. This is information technology serving relational ends.

> Zest for knowledge and a zeal for communicating it continue to be defining qualities of this agency. What's changed is that today the single-most effective tool we have for sharing and refining knowledge companywide is our intranet.

Truffles in its modern form was set up in 2003, including a robust search engine and a state-of-the-art interface:

> Combining cutting-edge technology with a visually compelling design, Truffles simultaneously connects and educates 11,000 employees in 474 offices. It enables Ogilvy to set one consistently high standard and deliver it globally. All of the agency's accumulated wisdom – its best practices and thought leadership – is just a click away. Best of all, this information is constantly updated and available from home, office, or on the road.[5]

2. Practise 360-degree staff appraisal

One relational system adopted by over 30,000 UK companies is serious staff appraisal that includes everyone up to top management. Set up in 1991 by the UK government, the Investors In People (IIP) standard has now developed into an internationally recognized quality accreditation.

The Aberdeen-based financial services firm Johnston Carmichael joined IIP because they believed it would 'help them to provide an even better client service, improve profits and increase motivation among the partners and employees'. According to the Training and Development Partner, Lesley Wilson, 'It has given us considerable kudos in the profession and confirms that our human resource systems are good enough to satisfy an external verifier... It has also improved communication among the partners and staff. Our training scheme has benefited in that the courses are better conceived, and evaluation is undertaken to ensure these have achieved their objectives.'

Since Johnston Carmichael achieved IIP, they have seen an increased number of employees undertake professional and vocational qualifications, allowing the partnership to extend its range of high-quality services to clients.

3. Consider whose decisions will be most effective

Management decisions don't need to be generated from overhead and then imposed.

A good example of relational proximity in decision-making is provided by Clive Woodward, who coached the English rugby union side that won the 2003 World Cup.

Woodward believed that team disciplines had to originate in the team. So when punctuality at training became a problem, he called the team together, explained what concerned him and then said, 'Now you know how I feel about it. What should I do?'

The players discussed it and came back with a recommendation. If someone arrives late for training, they said, he should be shut out. Woodward could have implemented the same rule himself, but it was far more effective through being thought up by the team. That way, latecomers were held accountable by their teammates – not by the coach.

A second issue arose when a couple of the players started

a slanging match in the press. Once again, Woodward called them together, explained his position and asked them to come up with a solution. It took three months, but eventually the team reached a common mind. They had to keep talking to the press, they said, because this provided an important source of income. But if anyone used a press interview to air grievances against another team member, that person should never play for England again.

The threat had to be carried out, recalled Woodward, only once.[6]

One large FTSE-100 telecommunications company employs a similar system of accountability. For conference calls, everybody must be present at least two minutes in advance. For face-to-face meetings, five minutes. And for larger corporate meetings, fifteen minutes. The team then decides what the appropriate 'punishment' will be if a person fails to meet the deadline.

4. At organizational level, adopt the Relational Business Charter

Some of the relational constraints in companies derive not from management practices but from the way companies are structured and go about their business.

The Relational Business Charter (RBC) is a proposal being explored by the Relationships Foundation. It provides a framework which existing companies can adopt, should the directors and shareholders agree to do so. No government regulation is required.

Adopting the RBC implies a commitment by a company in its constitution not only to maximize returns for investors but to seek higher levels of involvement from shareholders, employees, suppliers, customers and other stakeholders. Every line-item promotes relational proximity. Overall, the advantages to the company accrue in terms of perceived legitimacy, greater innovation, productivity, access to capital, sustainability and accountability.

The Charter itself is a simple ten-point statement of purpose, committing the company, with shareholder approval, to:

Relational Business Charter

1. Modify the goals of the company by including relational business objectives in its constitution.

2. Ensure proper training in the relational purpose and ethos of the company for shareholders, directors and employees.

3. Promote dialogue among all significant stakeholders – for example, by holding quarterly meetings for all stakeholders.

4. Encourage direct ownership of shares by individuals and families, in particular by ensuring that at least 25 per cent of equity is held by individuals and trustees of family trusts.

5. Incentivize all shareholders to maintain a long-term investment in the company – for example, to hold their shares for longer than three years.

6. Protect the family and community interests of employees, including a guarantee that all employees have one weekend day off per week and a maximum 48-hour week as under EU rules.

7. Demonstrate that the contributions of all employees are valued by keeping company pay differentials within a ten to one ratio (after tax, per hour worked).

8. Contribute to company financial stability by keeping the debt-to-equity ratio below three to one.

9. Ensure suppliers are treated fairly – for example, by paying them within thirty days.

10. Fulfil obligations to the wider community – for instance, by paying national and local taxes, and protecting the physical and social environment.

The RBC would need to be supported by a Relational Ratings Agency (RRA). Like a credit ratings agency, this would make an external assessment – but not of financial standing, rather of relationships among key stakeholders. It would use objective benchmarks from the RBC (for example, debt–equity ratio, level of pay differentials, working hours) and also analysis of the relationship ethos gained from a questionnaire filled in by the company. The published rating is to be available to investors, potential (and actual) employees, suppliers and other stakeholders. The RRA would also provide a Relational Business Forum as a resource for training and knowledge on relationship issues.

109

Relational Systems

CHAPTER 8

Relational Work–Life Balance

Work–life balance is one of the most talked-about relational issues today.

It's as well to be clear about the facts. And the facts are not encouraging. According to a 2007 study by Relationships Forum Australia, which looked at work patterns across the Western world and their impact on life at home:

> An emerging body of international research is showing that long and atypical working patterns are associated with dysfunctional family environments, including: a) Negative health outcomes for those working these times, particularly if they are parents, b) Strained family relationships, c) Hostile and ineffective parenting. And, critically, both long/ atypical hours and dysfunctional family environments are associated with: d) Reduced child wellbeing.
>
> Notably, these associations are evident when either or both parents work atypical schedules, so the timing of fathers' not just mothers' work matters to children.[1]

The fact that things are getting worse – and in Australia the impact of working hours on families is a national concern – itself reveals a lack of relational thinking at the level of economic policy. Two of the main drivers of longer and unsocial hours in business are the emergence of 'value-based management' (value

being assessed exclusively in terms of return to shareholders)
and the seven-day trading week.

If policymakers are unwilling or unable to contain the demands of the workplace, what can relational managers do?

First of all, understand the nature of the problem.

The weakness in work–life balance

The phrase 'work–life balance' suggests simply that work and life comprise two competing demands, so that work colleagues, clients, friends and family compete for the same scarce commodity – your time.

In reality, it feels a little more complicated than that. As work spills over from the nine-to-five day, we engage in an increasingly frantic effort to juggle and squeeze our non-work commitments into the remaining time. Things are made worse when work demands are unpredictable, and worse still when you and your partner both have to cope with busy and changing schedules and non-work life turns into an endless negotiation of family time, housework and childcare.

Something in our culture can make us feel almost apologetic for requesting time off from work simply to deal with family issues. And, consequently, we will find ourselves conducting all transactions (with the doctor, the children's teacher, the homeless person at the station) in a limited time frame and at high speed. Consequently also, we will feel pressure on our central, supportive relationships – ones with friends and family that often lie outside the workplace and can't be maintained adequately by sending an email every other day.[2]

A relational approach to work and life, however, begins from the observation that the non-work world is as important as the work world. The work world may pay the bills, but without adequate support from the non-work world, nobody is going to sustain good concentration and brilliant performance at the workplace. Work and life cannot realistically be seen as two self-contained and separate universes. They are heavily interlocked and interdependent.

In other words – for sound reasons and in practical ways – you have to prioritize life as seriously as work.

The drain of relationship time

The Bluewater shopping centre in Kent in the UK is a modern counterpart to Notre Dame. From the moment you leave your car in one of the 130,000 parking spaces, you know that this colossal blend of retailing and leisure puts you, the consumer, bang in the middle of the frame. As the developers say:

> The guests' experience has been enhanced by creating a sense of place including cultural elements and civic art, by creating attractive environments in which to eat and relax, by including internal and external landscapes, and redefining customer services and amenities.[3]

Note that at Bluewater you are a guest, not a shopper. Go there on Sunday and it's clear that shopping in the mega-mall is understood to be a *social* activity. People go there with friends or family. Many of them are wearing their best outfits. And the whole place has clearly been designed to encourage those positive emotions we associate with good company.

At the same time, however, Bluewater belongs to a commercial culture in which recreation of all kinds is tending to focus more and more on *individual* fulfilment. To some extent, all this is a side effect of increasing wealth. We now demand and expect that our individual preferences should be catered for. We want an exact fit. I buy a snowboard, you buy skis. Also, as technologies get cheaper, it becomes possible for individuals to buy, for personal use, equipment they'd previously have shared.

The growth in transport technology and electronic media has largely focused on individual use. According to the Census Bureau's American Community Survey, in 2007 three-quarters of workers in the USA were still driving to work, the number of carpoolers having dropped from 25 per cent to 10 per cent in the last two decades of the twentieth century.[4]

Meanwhile, in the UK, a survey commissioned in 2006 by Lloyds TSB Insurance found that seven in ten children have their own television, while 60 per cent have a personal games console. In a third of cases, the value of the gadgetry in children's bedrooms exceeded £2,000.[5]

On the positive side, you can say that this development gives you greater individual control and thus greater individual satisfaction. Also, individually controlled technologies such as text messaging have relational benefits. But there's a negative side, too, because the more you grow accustomed to entertaining yourself in solitude, the less effort you will put into making and sustaining relationships.

In a 2000 survey, roughly 4,000 American adults from 3,000 households reported that, since going online, they spent 8 per cent less time attending social events, 13 per cent less time with family and friends, and 26 per cent less time talking to people on the phone. Those who spent five to ten hours a week online reported a 25 per cent fall in social activity. They said they 'see fewer people, talk to fewer people, and go out less often'.[6]

If time is the currency of relationships, then the way we redeploy our time to accommodate new technologies is an issue deserving thought. Not only do unsocial hours make our leisure periods less likely to coincide: we are also tending to give a larger slice of our discretionary time to solo activities.

It's illuminating to see what happens when you try to reverse the pattern. For example, as research for a newspaper feature, reporter Diane Appleyard went cold turkey on technology – in this case, by locking up the family television for a week. The effects surprised her – and illustrate what kind of trade offs occur when you try to organize your life differently:

By the end of the TV-free week, I noticed a marked improvement in the children's attitude to each other and to me. It made them use their imagination to create fantasy games, such as dens. Beth read four books in the course of the week.

Charlotte learned several new card games, and we read lots of books together.

The house, however, is a tip. No TV means playing games and creating mess. I am also exhausted. The week made me realise how much I rely on the TV to get them out of my hair.

It is the literal equivalent of being able to put them both in a cupboard for a couple of hours.[7]

One of the reasons we don't notice the erosion of real relationships is the way the media draws us all up into that loose network of relationships that constitutes citizenship of the world. Like TV and the internet, radio in part acts as an information service connecting you to events in government, society, industry and the markets. You don't need to know anyone in the studio, and they certainly don't need to know you. To eavesdrop on the national gossip is enough.

It's a peculiarity of our media-intense culture that we can enjoy an imagined intimacy with complete strangers. Presenters on both TV and radio affect a personal manner, which suggests that the illusion of relationship matters to the media user's sense of inclusion in the wider community. It could be argued, in fact, that the media in general provides us with a set of 'surrogate family members' – celebrities we all feel we know and in whose stories we all have an interest. It's for this reason, presumably, that crowds of complete strangers register grief when media personalities die (British broadcaster Jill Dando, for example, or Diana, Princess of Wales). They've even been known to send flowers to television studios when familiar TV soap characters pass away in a programme.

In terms of hours and minutes per week, the media now occupies a significant position in most people's 'relational base'. It may or may not be a shared activity. But it is always qualitatively different from person-to-person relating, as anyone will know who has had the experience of finishing a busy day in a hotel room, alone except for the TV set.

Who matters most?

Refer back to your own relational base diagram. Which relationships did you place nearest to the centre? Who provides the anchor point of your life?

If you are married or in a long-term relationship, almost certainly your spouse or partner will be close to the middle. If so, this relationship needs special attention, not just because of its centrality but because the workplace and the surrounding culture expose it to many risks. It's where the rubber really hits the road in the work–life balance.

Home relationships are not usually an emphasis in business books. But, in relationship terms, work and non-work powerfully interconnect. In fact, one of the best things you can do for your business career is to invest heavily in your key relationship outside the workplace. If those relationships go wrong – if your kids get into trouble, if you go through a messy divorce – it's not going to boost your work performance. It will do very emphatically the opposite.

Note, though, that Western culture can be notably unsupportive in this, because so much attention is paid to how relationships begin and far less to how they sustain themselves over the ensuing years.

Romantic relationships may start out with a passionate conflagration – a whirlwind that picks you up and transports you. But as the relationship matures, passion ceases to be an outside force acting upon you and emerges as a quality sustained and furthered by your own actions.

When people say the passion has gone out of a relationship, almost always they mean that the spontaneous rush of love has evaporated and they now feel beached. But love isn't something you feel or get; it is something you *do*.

The island doctor in Louis de Bernières's novel *Captain Corelli's Mandolin* gives this advice to his daughter:

Love is a temporary madness, it erupts like volcanoes and
then subsides. And when it subsides you have to make
a decision. You have to work out whether your roots

have so entwined together that it is inconceivable that
you should ever part. Because this is what love is. Love
is not breathlessness, it is not excitement, it is not the
promulgation of promises of eternal passion, it is not the
desire to mate every second minute of the day, it is not lying
awake at night imagining that he is kissing every cranny of
your body. No, don't blush, I am telling you some truths.
That is just being 'in love', which any fool can do. Love is
what is left over after the being in love has burned away, and
this is both an art and a fortunate accident.[8]

In all but its opening phases, a relationship does not tip passion
out of the sky like rain. Once you're off the starting blocks, you
create passion in the relationship, not by putting your partner
on a pedestal but by deepening your mutual knowledge and
appreciation and constantly constructing the relationship by
putting the other's needs first.

Hard work? Yes – but it's almost certain you won't increase
the passion in your relationship any other way. Too often we get
to a point where we think we know the other person and even
take a perverse pride in being able to predict their responses.

This is a presumption and a damaging mistake. Your partner
is one of a kind; inexhaustible, irreplaceable, full of surprises,
and the source of all the passion you will ever want – if you
make the effort to get and stay close.

Perhaps you are reading this as your plane touches down.
You may be calculating that you have two hours to pick up your
four-year-old from the childminder, that tomorrow will largely
be swallowed up by shopping and chores, and that you and
your partner are probably so exhausted that you will sleep until
midday on Sunday, after which there will be just about time to
take the family to the park before evening descends and the
weekend is as good as over.

This is the real world into which we have to introduce some
serious thinking about how we organize our relationships.
And things may not be as they seem. Ironically, one of the
reasons some romantic relationships fail may be the very
conscientiousness with which the spouses/partners put their

children first. Christopher Vincent, a couples' psychiatrist
Tavistock Marital Studies Institute in London, warned re
of a danger 'that children will become emotionally handic
by parents whose primary investment is in their children
than each other'.

As a friend once put it, 'The most important thing a man can
do for his children is to love their mother.'

Premium relating

Where is the best place to build relationships with those you
live with?

One of the most important, and most effective, is the dinner
table.

To a large extent, the social group we call a household is
identified by the presence of its members around the dinner table.
As a base of 'plenary' rather than one-to-one communication,
the shared meal provides a unique chance to reinforce a sense
of membership, to reflect on recent events and to engage in
forward planning.

As a relational opportunity, it also carries some unusual
qualities – particularly in child-raising. For instance, because
there are fewer distractions, children are more likely to focus on
conversation. Unlike the hour before school, interaction with
parents will not be task-related, and this means children will
be more likely to feel comfortable offloading problems they're
going through with peers or school work. Hearing adults discuss
the day's events also gives children a window on the grown-
up world. It's in this processing of the day's events that your
values most clearly emerge. What you did or didn't do in a given
situation. What you thought of somebody else's action and how
you chose to respond to it.

Studies indicate that family meals produce long-term
benefits.

For example, psychologists Blake Sperry Bowden and Jennie
Zeisz recently studied the link between family eating and the
social problems of teenagers. They took a sample of 527 teenagers

and categorized each one as either 'well-adjusted' or 'not well-adjusted'. The 'well-adjusted' teens (less likely to take drugs or be depressed, more motivated at school, and with better peer relationships) ate with their families an average of five days a week. The 'not well-adjusted' group ate as a family only three days a week.[9]

And don't forget, of course, that eating with your children lets you nag them about eating those greens – not a frivolous point, since a Harvard Medical School survey of 16,000 nine-to fourteen-year-olds in the US found that 'kids who sit down to eat with their siblings and parents eat nearly a whole serving more of fruit or vegetables, per day, than those who rarely eat *en famille*... communal eaters consumed more iron and vitamins B6, B12, C and E'.[10]

Remember that a meal involves a collection of activities surrounding the preparation and eating of food. From a relational viewpoint, it can be successful even if your prize soufflé sinks – as long as people connect in conversation. Meals provide opportunities for shared tasks, for dividing up the cooking and mucking in with the washing-up. If your kitchen's large enough, it can easily become the social centre of the house – a place where people will hang around rather than disappearing to their own rooms.

We all face huge competition for time. Adults get back late from work. There's homework to be done. Somebody will have an absolutely must-see TV programme. On Tuesdays, somebody else will be out till eight o'clock at a gymnastics class. And so it goes on.

Not surprisingly, according to research conducted for Paxo, almost a quarter of UK families don't manage to eat together even once a week.[11] Unexpectedly, perhaps, technology seems to make this juggling of timetables even more difficult.

Food technology has kept up with – and in many ways facilitated – our changing lifestyle. We can only stagger the evening meal over two or three hours if we can serve reasonably varied and palatable food in small units – whether it's chicken tikka masala or a tin of beans.

In this way, food technology buys us time. Like other small

domestic miracles – hot plumbing, piped-in power, vacuum cleaners, washing machines – it claws back the hours we might have spent in unrewarding labour and gives them back to us to use at our discretion. Yet the relational effect can be negative.

A good example is the microwave oven. The genius of the microwave is to produce a wide range of cooked foods – and to do it in about as long as it takes you to untie your shoelaces. No risky stirring of white sauce. No agonizing wait. The microwave can do what even the most accomplished domestic cook cannot: turn out hot individual portions fast and efficiently and do it again and again and again.

But the microwave can also rearrange what we might call the 'unavoidable interactions' in the home. Buying a microwave doesn't prevent people eating together, of course. But if you can warm up macaroni cheese at seven, o'clock there's less pressure on you to get back home and share a pizza at six o'clock.

On one level, the technology is helping us cope with our time-pressured lifestyles and non-aligned schedules. On another level – and simultaneously – it is removing a reason to put relating time first.

Incidentally, the same is true of clearing away the dishes. A survey commissioned by the British supermarket giant Tesco revealed that 68 per cent of washers-up had been kissed at the kitchen sink.[12] The aphrodisiac effects of detergent? Sadly not. It just illustrates how the 'unavoidable' task of washing dishes after a meal offers an excuse to be with, and be close to, others we care about. Do we love washing up? No. Is it a good time to talk? Often, yes.

Conversation grows in this kind of soil. Sit someone down for the purpose of 'having a conversation', and you'll produce awkwardness. Work on a joint task that removes the necessity for eye contact and gives your hands something to do, and conversation will flow naturally.

Devices like microwaves and dishwashers, then, present us with more than one set of questions. We are used to asking: How much does it cost? Have I got room for it in my kitchen? Does it fit my colour scheme? How much can I fit inside it? But it's just as reasonable to ask: What effects might the use of this machine have on relationships? Is the time spent together on household tasks more usefully spent on individual pursuits? If I buy this machine, how do I preserve household conversation?

Ways to implement relational work–life balance

Pressure on working hours has increased. Christmas in many homes remains almost sacrosanct as family time, but Sunday as a joint recreation day is much less universal than it was. For many in retail and related professions, market pressure to relax restraints on Sunday trading has made it increasingly difficult to spend shared time with others. Contrary to popular belief, this problem doesn't affect only families and shopworkers. Your Sunday morning five-a-side football might be disrupted by weekend working. And this is now just as likely to happen to lawyers, accountants, librarians and health professionals.[13]

Work–life balance is an issue for you and for the people who work under you.

The relational manager will have more or less influence over company policy depending on the organization. But it may be worth raising options on working hours that could make your staff more productive through putting more of their time under their own control.

For example, how much room is there for flexitime? What precedents have been set in this area? When does the organization really need people to be there, and when could they work more effectively from home? Is a four-day week an option? Flexible working arrangements – including flexitime, part-time work, job-sharing, shift-swapping, working from home and team-based self-rostering – are increasingly being considered as options by employers seeking to attract and retain quality staff.[14]

An investment banker in the City of London recently agreed with his boss to work nine out of ten working days in every two weeks, thus freeing up every second Friday to walk his children to school and spend the day with his wife. He had to work hard

to convince his boss, and accept a drop in salary, but the benefits
were huge. Similarly, a woman in senior management at a large
UK charitable organization uses the existing flexibility on hours
to work longer Monday to Thursday so she can take off Friday
afternoons and extend her weekend.

For your own initiatives in dealing with the work–life balance,
consider the following.

1. Measure home activities in terms of relational value

Clearly some activities – including most sports – are inherently
social. You can't play football on your own. That said, different
issues arise depending on whether you play for your company
team (thus reinforcing work relationships) or play for a side
whose other members you're unlikely to see except out on the
field.

How relational is your use of television and computers? Do
individual members of the household watch programmes of
their own choosing, or do you organize viewing events – a movie
or live sports – that everyone could share in? Quality isn't the
issue. The latest Dickensian costume drama and the latest tragic
twist in *EastEnders* both have relational value if they becomes
grist in the mill of tomorrow's conversation.

What about your choice of channels? Does having 240
channels to choose from give you relational pay-offs, or do you
waste more time and have more difficulty finding something
everybody wants to see?

There's also the matter of using activities to draw in other
people. For example, you can walk on your own or you can
walk in company. You can wash your car at the filling station
or you can wash it yourself out on the street where you may get
interrupted by talkative neighbours and inquisitive children.

Even pets have relational value. A dog in a family acts as
a catalyst, provoking action and interaction, and as a symbolic
device, providing a conversational starter with other dog-walkers.
It becomes an intermittent focus of attention and conversation.
And, like a child, it has the ability to interrupt and surprise. Try
as you may, you won't get that kind of relational input from your
cyberpet.

2. Experiment by writing out a relational time-budget

A lot of busy middle-income parents have tried to ring-fence the time they spend in direct, hands-on child-rearing. Unfortunately, research evidence simply does not support the pious hope that 'quantity-time' taken away from kids can be compensated for by short, high-velocity 'quality time', by handing out PlayStations and mobile phones, or by professional caring.[15]

In the end, there's just no substitute for 'being there' on a pretty regular basis. And the older a child gets, the less discretion you have in setting the timetable. If you're not available the moment your sixteen-year-old wants to unload on you, the opportunity for that important parent–child heart-to-heart chat could be gone for ever.

Relationship time is hard to divide up into regular slots, and you work within limitations. Nevertheless, it's important to start your thinking from 'How much time do I need to put into this?' and not 'How much time can I spare from work at the end of the week?' You are far less dispensable in your role as a partner and parent than you are in your role as employee.

If you wrote out a relational time-budget, what would the big items of expenditure be, and why?

For many couples, the main difficulty is that the pressures of life give them little time to spend exclusively with each other. They are left with the residue of the day or the weekend. One way round this is to set aside 'couple days' well in advance so that once a month both partners drop all domestic chores, work obligations and other commitments, and simply focus on their relationship with each other. It probably requires getting out of the house and away from piles of paper, laundry, DIY, dishes and other distractions. In the end, there is no substitute for a solid block of quality time spent with each other if the relationship is to survive the pressures of married life. We ignore such disciplines at our peril.

What matters isn't just the amount of time you spend with those who are closest to you, but *when* you spend it. Hitting the special occasions will multiply the impact by a factor of ten. Taking your partner out on their birthday – and not the day after. Being present for your son's sports day (often a never-to-

be-repeated occasion). Being there to see your daughter receive
her prize at the school prize-giving. Next day just won't do.

3. Think why you're going on holiday
In relationship terms, large blocks of free time are a bit like large lump sums of cash. You have to decide how to spend them.

Although the brochures seldom say it outright, holidays aren't just about seeing new things, eating exotic foods or lying on a warm, remote beach. The fourteen days you spend on vacation are one of your most valuable relating opportunities.

So who do you go with? Taking a tour with strangers is, of course, a good way of 'meeting people', especially for singles with room in their lives to make new friends and keep up with them. Alternatively, the institution of the 'family holiday' provides a means of building up *existing* relationships. For two weeks, the nuclear family group gets to spend recreational time together in a setting more stimulating and relaxed than the working week at home.

But, even here, it's worth thinking through the details. Which relationships are most needing time? It may be a relief for parents to offload the kids on to the hotel children's club, but is that helping you relate as a family? Presumably, you don't want to get back from Tenerife and find your children remembering more about the club leader than they remember about you. And how do you use the time with your partner when the kids are off at their beach volleyball lessons? Is it time used in building your relationship or time spent sunbathing?

Of course, you don't have to take your holiday off the peg. It's possible, for example, to use holiday time for visiting family rather than isolating yourselves on a distant beach. It's possible to team up with friends. And it's possible to go on a retreat and spend the time completely alone – giving you future relational benefits through being able to recuperate and recharge your batteries.

4. Plan more than the menu at mealtimes
Family dinner may be premium relating time, but, just like any other area of life, meals can be an arena for bad relating.

People drag to the dinner table much of the emotional baggage of their day. Which may mean you'll want to think through in advance the kinds of interaction that are likely to take place.

Fairly obviously, it helps conversation if you are sitting around a table facing one another. Yes, watching the news can be educational but, in relationship terms, having the TV on at mealtimes may represent a wasted opportunity.

In family situations, you are one of the presiding adults and can therefore set the rules and act as the chairperson. Mealtimes are generally not a good time to bring up disciplinary issues or uncompleted homework – not least because this 'public' setting will produce shaming rather than creative motivation.

Consider turning off the mobile phone and turning on the answering machine – moves that will not only save you from distractions but demonstrate clearly how you value and prioritize mealtimes. And if people in your home have a habit of not turning up when you call them, try ringing a bell!

A senior executive once confided, 'You know, I would never go to a board meeting without spending several hours reading the papers carefully and thinking through what I'm going to say. If you pressed me, I would have to say that I regard the time that I spent with my teenagers over dinner as more significant from a long-term point of view than any board meeting. However, I spent no time at all thinking through in advance what we would discuss over dinner, and no time reflecting afterwards about who said what around the table.'

In business, we routinely lay out agendas and guide discussions. Yet, in the personal arena, we let conversation proceed in a haphazard manner, with no particular objective in mind. If we go to the trouble of creating shared time together over a meal, it stands to reason that we will want to use that time well. And good conversation doesn't just spring out of the air.

Family conversations have a habit of becoming self-fuelling if you can only get them off the launch pad. Almost anything will do as a starter, provided it engages interest and doesn't make people feel they're being interrogated. Ask people around the table what they like or detest, what they'd do if they had a million pounds, whether they think it's a good idea to buy a chimpanzee as a pet.

Variety enlivens interaction. People can 'dine out' on a good story because what they have to say transports their listeners into unknown places, arouses curiosity, sparks imagination. Theodore Zeldin, a passionate exponent of the art of conversation, believes that 'humanity is a family which has hardly met. One of the best ways it can meet is for our traditions of family hospitality to be revived.' And if you can't bring newcomers in, let the novelty of the world be transmitted through the excursions of family members. The family, says Zeldin,

> ... may treat itself as a base from which its members set out to explore the outside world, and to which they return with something new to say, so that conversation is constantly enriched by outside as well as inside happenings... It is by conversations with others, by mixing different voices with our own, that we can turn our individual life into an original work of art.[16]

In contrast, one seventeen-year-old sees clearly what's going on at his family dinner table:

> Dad never really listens. Mum has to take centre-stage without being interrupted. I think it's legitimate to interrupt: it shows interest. It's better with my friends because they treat me as a peer, and they get impassioned about things, which parents don't. A conversation should be fuelled by the passion that we have for the subject.[17]

CHAPTER 9

Relational Travel

Even in the age of mass telecommunications, your relationships remain anchored in the physical location of other people. And that means travel surrounds you with strangers.

On business trips, you will find yourself in a range of contexts in which you have a lot of face-to-face meetings (including some very long meetings with your seat partners on a long-haul flight) but in relationships that score low in time, knowledge, parity and shared purpose. In fact, the need to establish these things largely explains why you are travelling.

Consequently, alongside the normal disruptions to schedule and routine, there is likely to be a far greater relational distance between you and those you interact with than is normal in the course of your daily work. If close relationships were oxygen, you'd be operating in pretty thin atmosphere. And this presents two separate challenges: first, the challenge of building effective new relationships in your travel location; and, second, the challenge of maintaining – and, in some cases, not sabotaging – your key supporting relationships at home.

Working with strangers

A businessman arrived at a London terminus brought to near standstill by emergency rail inspections. This extended his forty-minute journey home to nearly three hours. But what struck him was the speed with which the shared inconvenience – and thus the shared goal of leaving the place as soon as possible – opened up conversations with other passengers. It began with general complaints and jokes about the railways but soon led to more serious conversation and even to offers of help.

Occasionally, a little enforced relational proximity encourages us to 'open up' to people we don't know and with whom we would normally have no reason to start a conversation. But this is unusual. Moving through public space today – streets, metros, stations, airports – confronts you with vast numbers of real live strangers, and we spend most of our time screening them out.

We anticipate certain interactions and either prepare for them or avoid them. We know how to handle the checkout encounter. We know the way to say sorry if we blunder into a fellow traveller. And we scan the horizon to avoid people handing out flyers and shaking paper cups.

There is a cost to engaging with strangers in unscripted situations. We may end up parting with money. We will certainly have to part with time. There is a danger we may be made to look foolish. In the early 1990s, a UK TV documentary team hired an actress to collapse in a busy street and then filmed the consequences. They were in an urban shopping mall and nobody stopped for *forty-five minutes*.[1]

This basically defensive attitude – in which the norm and the aim are *not* to relate – is reinforced by a sense of competition. Get stuck at a busy junction and it won't be long before you start to feel a little exasperated with the driver in front who's marooned himself in the middle of it. Or consider your attitude to the person who somehow slips ahead of you in that mile-long queue at the airport check-in.

This ability to isolate ourselves relationally is a survival technique and, to some extent, culturally defined. But the reflex of avoiding encounters with people we don't know can impose limitations, since the strangers who potentially threaten to delay us or interrupt our day are also potentially undiscovered sources of new information and contacts.

One of the authors had just stepped off a flight from Nairobi and was standing bleary-eyed at 5.30 a.m., waiting for his luggage to come round on the carousel at Gatwick Airport. He noticed that the person standing next to him had luggage with a Cambridge label on it and decided to ask him if he was going back there. He said he was. A minute's conversation revealed that this fellow traveller was Dr Belbin, head of a company assessing team-building relationships in corporates. Belbin introduced his wife and offered the author a lift back to Cambridge. This not only saved a lot of time and trouble but provided the opportunity to learn a great deal about relationship processes in team-building.

What do you radiate?

Every friend you have was once a stranger.

So how do you come across to those who don't know you? When someone glances at you sitting on a train, what exactly do they see? And when you're introduced to a new business acquaintance, what do they experience within the first ten seconds of meeting you? Observed in a meeting by a third party what kind of person do you appear to be?

For most of us, the answer is that it rather depends what mood we're in. When we feel good, we tend to be more outgoing, more ready to smile and talk. We radiate energy and invite engagement. Conversely, when we feel tired or distracted, we tend to withdraw. Our energy level goes down and we disengage.

It is quite possible, though, to commit to behaving in such a way that others will usually want to move into your space. You don't have to be an extrovert or a natural talker to greet others with a smile and look them in the eye. Or to make a discipline out of remembering names and one or two personal details. Simple things like this are the basis of real influence.

Dr John Edmund Haggai, founder of the Haggai Institute for Advanced Leadership Training, has devoted his life to relationship-building and tells some striking stories about its effects:

In 1981, I returned to the lovely island of Bali in Indonesia. Since rooms were tight, I did not stay at my usual stopping place, the Bali Intercontinental, but instead secured accommodations at the Bali Hyatt.

When I arrived and started up the steps to the entrance, the head bellman said, 'Welcome to the Bali Hyatt, Dr Haggai. We have reserved the Presidential Suite for you.'

I protested that I had reserved a minimum rate single room.

But he said, 'The General Manager insists. He wants you to charge everything to the room – your laundry, dry cleaning, meals, telephone – everything. You are his guest.'

It was one of the most elegant accommodations I had seen in all of my world travels.

Within minutes, the General Manager, Michael Ou, arrived to greet me. Stunned, I tried to express my thanks.

'You don't remember me, do you?' he said.

I had to confess I didn't.

He said, 'In the 1960s when you stayed at the Singapore Intercontinental, I was a bellman, hustling bags. Every time you came, you treated me just as grandly as you treated your friend, the General Manager, George Milne. I have harbored a secret dream for all these years that some day I would run my own hotel and be able to show you gratitude for the encouragement and inspiration you gave me.'[2]

How far do we use our daily encounters with other people to do something constructive? Busy managers on high-pressure business trips are apt to treat service staff as instant problem-solvers or people on whom they can vent their frustration with a system that's let them down. Busy relational managers might be able to find a better way.

Life in the relational vacuum

Refer back to your relational base diagram in Chapter 1. You stand at the centre of the circles. You rely on the people you have marked around you on the diagram. But they also rely on you. So when you move to another place for an extended period of time, two things happen, which are represented here in Diagram 6.

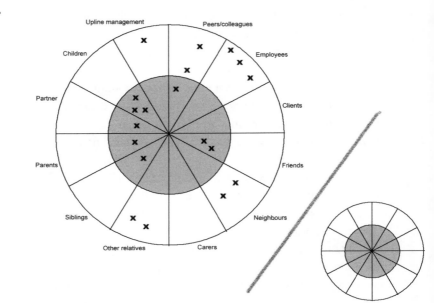

DIAGRAM 6: The traveller's relational base

The first thing is that those close to you at home are forced to function without you. The jobs they rely on you to do have to be done by somebody else. If you have a partner and family, this may open up a range of extra tasks – rides to school, shopping, child-management, looking after children while the other parent is out – that fall entirely on your partner.

The other thing that happens is you have to operate outside your nexus of supportive relationships. Yes, they are available electronically by email or video or phone. One executive who travels frequently will always up a twenty-four-hour live webcam link between his laptop and his living room. It enables him to see and, to some extent, interact with his children, wherever he can pick up a wi-fi signal, and creates a sense of participation in family life even when he is on the other side of the world. But, even so, the link is intermittent and fragmentary. In relational terms, the level of connectivity remains low. It only supports him to a degree.

One result of this isolation is that men, particularly, become vulnerable to sexual advances. And this happens at exactly the same moment as they are being targeted by the commercial sex industry – either through online or hotel cable porn or through the increasingly pervasive outlets for prostitution.

This might seem tangential to management. But, relationally, it is a crucial issue. Remember, relationships at home make or break performance at work. And for the many business people with partners and families, the fallout from pursuing another relationship, or of simply becoming a sexual cheat, can be considerable, even if they succeed in keeping the activity secret.

Nothing freezes a relationship more quickly than one partner's loss of confidence in the other – the suspicion, even the faintest thought, that they might not be playing straight. It kills spontaneity because you can only open yourself to another person if that other person is doing the same with you. For deceiver and deceived alike, the magic of shared trust simply dissolves. You are one person, not two. What does it say about you if, the moment the constraints are removed, you start to do things that would shame you were your close family to find out about them?

Ways to implement relational travel

For the relational manager, the goal in relational travel is to function in the same way at home and abroad, whether you are in the middle of your supportive relationships or distant from them. And that involves taking account not just of your own situation but of those you are responsible for.

1. Consciously build a relational base camp

Generally, being left behind is harder than going, especially if you are being left with responsibilities of the household and children. So, the first thing to do is check your domestic calendar for kids' school holidays, prize-givings, sports days, parents' evenings and so on, as this largely determines your partner's ability to cope when you're away. If you can possibly avoid it, don't leave too much to do until the last week, as this will prevent you spending unpressurized time with your partner and family before you leave on a lengthy trip.

Keeping in touch while you're away may not be easy. You may have to make calls late at night. There may be a long time difference. It may feel more like a duty than a pleasure. Nevertheless, try as far as you can to fit around your partner's schedule. Ringing just before dinner time may not set up the best conversation. And be prepared to tackle, rather than sideline, questions about household management. Trouble with the car or with the children's homework may seem insignificant in comparison to the multi-million-pound business dealings you are trying to pull off. But if it's important to your partner, it's important to you.

At the other end of the trip, leave time to listen to your partner and catch up properly on what's happened in your absence. Readjustment takes time. If you've been away for two or three weeks, a new routine will have been established in the house, and your partner will have taken over some of your roles. Last but not least, buying gifts for your kids is usually a no-brainer – but make sure you know what language of love your partner responds to. If you're a man, be aware that perfume isn't necessarily the best solution.

Some of the same issues arise with your team at the office. Things are going to come up when you're away – some anticipated, some not. And you don't necessarily want to be running office business back at the base from your BlackBerry.

So one thing to do before you leave is provide adequate briefing for staff left behind before you travel. Anticipate any issues that may arise, and make clear the lines of authority and decision-making in your absence. Even though you're not in regular contact with team members, you may want to maintain greater continuity with your 2i/c via a daily business call.

When you get back, allow the team opportunity to debrief. Show interest in their decisions and discoveries, and appreciation for what they've achieved without you being there. And don't forget that bringing back a few goodies gives you a good excuse to go round the office re-establishing contact individually with your team members.

2. Think through the relational fixed points for the trip

Business trips vary. You may be on your own or with a team. You may be meeting old acquaintances or people you've never met before. Whatever the situation, take a moment to think it through in terms of relationships.

Who are the people you'll spend your time interacting with? Who is the desk clerk at the hotel? Who is the contact person at the conference or in the company you've gone to visit? Who are the people you'll be keeping in contact with back home via phone or Skype? Make sure you think in terms of real people with real names and not just functions.

Doing this establishes the fact that you are never travelling entirely alone. These people may not be close like friends and family, but they are the fixed points in your relational world while you travel.

3. Respect the relational needs of others travelling on business

When you send others away, consider their relational needs. Complaints about internet links not working are more important than they seem, as internet provides one of the easiest and cheapest means of contact with those back home. It's inconvenient to miss a couple of days' emails, but not having the means to make cheap calls will reduce a person's interaction with family and deepen their sense of isolation. Make it your business to ensure that staff on business trips have onboard wireless with the right software and are staying at hotels that provide a free signal.

4. Keep fidelity on the agenda with your partner

Somewhere in the complexities of modern gender etiquette, there is a point where gentle banter with another person will be taken as an explicit come-on – whether you mean it that way or not.

One of the choices you may want to make concerns where to set boundaries: situations you won't put yourself in; advances you won't tolerate; subjects you won't talk about; ways in which you signal – discreetly but clearly – that you are not available and not to be messed with. If you decide in advance what you will and will not do, and stand by that commitment, you remain in control.

If you feel particularly vulnerable sexually, discuss this with your partner before you go and give them unlimited permission to call you on your mobile phone at any time of day or night. This isn't as hard as it sounds. If you communicate to your partner 'I want you to know that I have no room in my life for anyone but you', this powerfully reinforces the bond between you.

Fidelity can be a serious turn-on.

5. Be the perfect host

And don't forget what it's like the other way around when visitors or new recruits come into your relational circle. How effectively do you ease others into your own social group and get new relationships off the ground?

Many schools will help a new student integrate by assigning them a 'buddy' – another student whose job it is to act as host, contact point and source of information. The chair at a meeting will formally introduce the visitor. The host or hostess at the cocktail party will attach the new arrival to a conversational group, dropping a compliment or two as a way of giving the newcomer a profile.

Nuances are important. There are matters of etiquette – for example, do you introduce Michael Jackson to President Obama, or President Obama to Michael Jackson? Also, you don't want to communicate the feeling that the visitor is being consumed by the group, as though he or she mattered only as a boost to attendance figures or as an addition to the mailing list.

Some seemingly innocuous things can make a huge difference. As a man, offering to collect a visiting contact from the airport might look like a nice personal touch. But if the contact is a woman, being driven from airport to hotel by a man she's only lightly acquainted with may signal intentions on your part that are not going to set your business relationship off on the right footing.

Being a stranger – that is, without supportive relationships – in a meeting, in a company or in a country creates vulnerability. The stranger has no 'place'. And, for that reason, people in this position appreciate hugely any effort others make to include them and make them feel valued.

Relational Conflict Resolution

Visit www.office-politics.com and you'll find a lot of people complaining.

Here's one example:

> I have been with my company for a little over 1 year and I love my job. My boss, however, is a different story. He has been with the company for over 15 years and has been pulling the wool over everyone's eyes. I have caught him in several lies, stealing and harassing. He has generally just been exhibiting unethical behavior for a very long time. I went through my chain of command and requested to be pulled out from under his supervision because I just could not take it any longer. My request was granted. I now report to his boss. Now he is talking about me to everyone. He has been going to other managers/co-workers and making very nasty and just untrue statements about me in a professional capacity. It is just gossip, pure and simple.[1]

The fact that a contract ties you into certain relationships in the workplace might suggest that problems such as bullying result from too much relational proximity. In fact, it's usually the reverse. Just because you share a department or an office space doesn't mean there is much shared story among the team, or that people know one another well in contexts outside work, or that there is any strong sense of shared purpose. And the need for a reporting structure in larger corporations usually has the effect of weakening parity as a ground for mutual respect.

Relational managers take workplace conflict seriously because broken relationships will tend to break everything else, including productivity and profit.

They will also not hesitate to resort to disciplinary procedures should these be required. But it's important to realize that procedures have limitations. There is a high probability of making the relationship permanently dysfunctional. The impact on workplace morale is likely to be negative. In addition, those attempting to manage the process may find themselves damaging relationships further.

For example, a manager who ends up laying off an employee will usually consider the possibility of sabotage. So he will often opt to surprise the employee with the layoff notice, ask him to clear out his office straight away, and have someone escort him off the premises. That done, the manager may heave a sigh of relief that the employee hasn't been able to take out his resentment on the furniture or the computer system. The employee, however, who in most cases wouldn't have vented in this way, leaves the company believing he's been treated like a criminal and feels a stronger motivation to bad-mouth his former employer and perhaps sue for unfair dismissal.

So relational management will always look first at the relationships themselves and seek ways to turn them around before they reach crisis point. And, as with conflict of all kinds, that confronts you with the issue of forgiveness.

The forgiving path

'Forgive and forget', the proverb says blithely. But the whole problem with the past is that you *can't* forget as an act of will. The wrong done to you yesterday – by your boss, by your partner, by your friend or, for that matter, by a whole class of people such as 'the government' or 'criminals' – has changed you for ever. It is an event in your life story. And its psychological or material impact may be apparent for years ahead.

When these crises crop up – and sooner or later they will, in almost any setting – you have only three alternatives:

◆ You can live with conflict (the bad marriage, the worker enduring a tyrannical boss, the cold war).

◆ You can pull out (divorce, resignation, ethnic cleansing).

◆ Or you can set out to tackle the problem.

Forgiving may be a virtue, but only a fool would expect you to do it as a matter of routine. Almost by definition, we see forgiving wrongdoers – and especially serious wrongdoers – as going some considerable distance beyond the call of duty. There's also a sense in which *not* forgiving is integral to justice. The lasting determination to remember war crimes, for example, has been instrumental in the success of trials, even fifty years after the crimes occurred.

To the extent that a wrong is an assault on the moral order, then, it matters that justice is done. But to the extent that a wrong is an assault on a *relationship*, the best outcome may lie in another direction – not in retribution but in reconciliation.

After all, deciding *not* to forgive exacts its own cost. If your boss gives you a public tongue-lashing, you'll suffer a certain amount of damage to your ego. But you'll sustain a lot more damage if you nurse a grudge. Bitterness may feel like the next best thing to vengeance, but you might as well have a migraine for all the damage it's going to do to its intended target. Studies repeatedly underline the link between repressed anger and alcoholism, ill health and sometimes fatal stress on other relationships.

Place this sort of social pathology in the context of a business or public service and there are compelling reasons to take forgiveness seriously.

Organizationally, you don't need many people who can't or won't forgive each other – in the sense of properly resolving past wrongs – before you have a serious problem on your hands.

Resentful employees underperform, spread dissatisfaction and may deliberately undermine operations. There are simply too many sensitive relationships in an organization, and too much at stake in terms of company profitability and quality of service, to risk this kind of damage to the relational architecture.

The same is true in the political realm. Events in Kosovo, Northern Ireland, South Africa, Rwanda and the Middle East have brought the issue of forgiveness abruptly on to the political agenda.

According to the political commentator Donald W. Shriver Jr:

> If the conflict-ridden and conflict-prone peoples of the earth
> are to move away from a Hobbesian 'war of all against
> all' into forms of politics that are not merely war by other
> means, we must do something about the memories and
> the continuing legacies of the harms we have inflicted
> on each other in the recent or remote past... A major
> 'something' that we have to enact is a social, political form
> of forgiveness.[2]

Broken relationships have their skirts caught in the doors of history – and they can remain dysfunctional for an astonishingly long time. In international political terms, the Battle of the Boyne and the Crusades both provide mental 'back-markers' that have fuelled a whole string of later exchanges and thus entrench animosity and perpetuated struggle.

At some point in conflict situations, you have to let the past go, which, in the office context, means you have to stop yourself compiling a mental dossier against a person who's hurt you. It's not easy; you may have to remind yourself every day that you've decided to close this particular book. But it's only by demonstrating this kind of inner determination that relationships can be turned around.

Forgiveness and reconciliation

To some extent, workplace conflict is inevitable and can even be a creative driver. Organizations provide the arena for teamwork, but also for competition. And management hierarchies introduce into the workplace an element of relational distance that requires careful handling.

On top of the normal stresses and strains, we find, locked into the structures of big organizations, malfunctioning managers. In most cases, they are not bad people in any general sense, but their management style generates friction. Their bosses may be completely unaware of it. In fact, their apparently tough, no-nonsense attitude may be mistaken for efficiency. Yet these individuals can be quietly draining performance and value from the organization through high turnover, distraction, absenteeism and ineffectiveness. They are a problem that needs fixing.

How you go about this depends, first of all, on where you stand: as someone on the receiving end of bad management, as someone accused of dishing it out or as the senior manager called in to sort out a dispute further down the line.

Clearly, forgiveness is not the same as reconciliation. Forgiving is a unilateral act; reconciliation requires the cooperation of both parties. Nor is it a simple, self-contained or one-off event. A person makes a decision to forgive as part of the process of rebuilding a relationship. It's pulling the ripcord on a plummeting connection. And it's a step that needs total commitment.[3] Nevertheless, the willingness to forgive – to stop telling the story of your grievance over and over again, to yourself and others – must be present before reconciliation can take place.

It's important to recognize too that relationship breakdown also occurs outside the workplace – in homes and communities – and that involvement in this will impact a person's ability to handle things at work. Though nuanced, the same issues arise in conflict resolution in every arena – even between nations – and much the same relational principles apply.

Ways to implement relational conflict resolution

A large part of the task here is to establish a business culture that raises relational proximity within the organization or department and thus reduces the opportunities for conflict to take hold. This may mean, for example, taking time to integrate a new team member. New appointments can unsettle people. They may fear that the new person is going to encroach on their professional territory and thus put their employment under threat. So it's important to explain why the new person has been brought in and what their role is in light of current targets.

More generally, there are a number of relational approaches to handling conflict in the workplace.

1. Establish an atmosphere where sorry is good

In his simple and disarming book *Ten Powerful Phrases for Positive People,* Amway co-founder Rich DeVos singles out 'I was wrong' and 'I'm sorry' as the two most effective and, at the same time, most difficult things to say.[3]

The difficulty perhaps explains why it's so rare to hear an unqualified 'sorry' in the competitive corporate world. Most apologies take the form of 'I'm sorry, but…' which, in reality, turns them into exercises in self-justification. 'I'm sorry, but I wasn't informed…' 'I'm sorry, but I've been let down by the suppliers…' And so on. Nobody wants to take responsibility, for fear of appearing to be a ball-dropper and a weak link.

There's nothing wrong with backing down slowly and checking the facts before carrying the can. But mistakes are a fact of life. The most important thing is not to assign blame but to figure out what went wrong. If people rush to blame each other, there's something amiss with the corporate culture. Teams dominated by fear of reprimand will seldom take creative risks and will tend to underperform as a result.

For this reason, relational management aims for a sense of shared responsibility and an acceptance that things sometimes go wrong. In that setting, there's not much to add when the person who makes a mistake says, 'Sorry, I messed up.' It's hard to argue with an apology.

The director of a UK think tank asked his PA to phone through the number of guests expected for a meeting at 10 Downing Street as each required a pass. Owing to the pressure of work, she failed to make the call. Next morning she called the director to inform him of the error, then called Number 10 to apologize. No damage was done and nobody thought the worse of her.

2. Observe the rule of parity

Author David Augsburger tells the story of a counsellor who'd slept with two of his clients. Finally, he was discovered and had to confess to his wife. He miserably – and sincerely – pleaded for her forgiveness, but she refused to give it. Not, though, for the reason you'd think. She told him:

> No, I will not forgive you. I do not want the kind of relationship with you in which you are the offender and I am the forgiver. I don't want you grateful and indebted to me for the rest of our lives. I want us to work through this until we both understand our parts in the problem, until we can accept each other... You did the active part. I did the passive part in helping create a relationship that was open to outside invitations. Let's work it out until we're back together.[4]

Perhaps not all such breakdowns can be so neatly salvaged. But note the role played here by parity. In a situation where one person admitted their fault, the weight of moral advantage immediately piles up on the other side. If that is allowed to continue, the relational gap will become a hazard to both parties. Sooner or later the offender will tire of their role as debtor in the relationship, and further breakdown will ensue.

This is not to say that responsibility for every crisis in a relationship – at home or in the workplace – can be split down the middle. Sometimes one party will behave abysmally with no obvious provocation from the other. But being wronged does not make you irreproachable. And, in many workplace conflicts, both sides will contribute.

This is sometimes overlooked, partly because so much emphasis in the literature is placed on unprovoked bullying and partly because the shortcomings of managers can be more visible than the shortcomings of employees.

In either case, you can only effect reconciliation with the buy-in of both parties and by being careful to maintain parity, and therefore the grounds for respect, between the two. This includes a mutual willingness to identify and acknowledge the wrong. It's important the person wronged doesn't exaggerate the claims they are making. It's equally important not to understate them.

This isn't unusual. Young victims of child abuse, for example, may fear reprisals or simply feel too ashamed to acknowledge what's gone on. Many more of us are guilty of overlooking bullying, advantage-taking and rudeness in order to avoid 'causing a scene'. We tell ourselves we're forgiving another person's conduct, when what we're really doing is practising denial and avoidance – reclassifying the incident as inconsequential.

3. Manage people, not problems
The less relational proximity exists between team members, the more likely it is that you will see a colleague as one of the following:

◆ a vehicle – a means to obtaining something

◆ an obstacle – a hindrance to obtaining something

◆ an irrelevance – not important to your targets and therefore not worth your time.

Interest groups within offices not infrequently relate to one another on these terms. If your agenda involves changing company marketing, you will tend to see proponents of existing methods as obstacles to that agenda. If you are fixated on achieving promotion, you will tend not to build relationships with people whose influence cannot be turned in your favour.

Relational management resists seeing people in these instrumental terms. A team is, in the first instance, an assemblage of people, not an assemblage of skill-sets or agendas. You build team strengths from the unique combination of people you bring together. And, equally, when you have to sort out a dispute, you focus on the people involved, not simply on the complaints and the procedure.

Even the 'manager from hell' is not a lost cause. Archbishop Desmond Tutu, who chaired South Africa's Truth and Reconciliation Commission, provides some perspective on corporate management when he reminds us that:

> There are people in South Africa who have committed the most unbelievable atrocities, and I am willing for their deeds to be labelled with the harshest epithets: monstrous, diabolical, even devilish. However, monstrous deeds do not turn the perpetrators into monsters. A human person does not ultimately lose his or her humanity, which is characterised by the divine image in which every individual is created... The premise underlying the commission is that it is possible for people to change...[5]

Distinguishing the person from the action is the first step towards reconciliation. Bad management in corporations often arises not through calculated malice but through misunderstanding, ineptitude, insecurity and laziness. If a manager is failing, it's worth asking why. Is it simply a matter of inexperience? Can the problem be addressed through training? Are there conflicts of character and outlook that could be avoided by reassigning one of the people involved? Are there background issues outside the workplace that turn small anxieties and disagreements into crises?

The person, not the problem, is usually the key.

4. If you have to fire people, fire them relationally

Workplace conflict may finally result in you having to release a member of staff. Alternatively, in an economic downturn, the organization may be forced to downsize. Either way, you are faced with one of the manager's least pleasant jobs: breaking the bad news of redundancy.

The first thing to understand here is that you won't necessarily be forced into the position of carrying out an execution on somebody else's orders.

A UK, Oxford-based IT company was told recently by its American parent that it had to shed eight jobs in order to avoid closure. The story got around the offices and soon the staff asked the manager for a consultation. They proposed that, in order to avoid redundancies, everyone in the company be offered the chance to accept a 20 per cent pay cut.

Now in a mediating role, the manager took the proposal back to the US parent. They responded with disbelief. Why, they asked, would you put yourself through indefinite pain just to 'save your eight worst people'? The assumption that cuts would hit the 'eight worst' employees (as opposed to the eight in a department without current orders or whose jobs could most easily be sacrificed in the short term) is blinkered, to say the least. Nevertheless, the parent group consented to honour such an agreement on condition of a 100 per cent buy-in.

The Oxford company held a secret ballot, with options of reducing pay by 5 per cent, 10 per cent and 20 per cent. In the end, all failed because three employees refused to take any cut at all. However, the fact of management and workforce having participated in an effort to save jobs ultimately made the redundancy a less traumatic process.

Secondly, there is the matter of how you understand your role as manager.

Gallup's analysis of management style notes the belief of many managers that 'with enough willpower and determination, virtually all behaviours can be changed'. This has an unfortunate kickback. If the employee, despite ongoing support, encouragement, incentive and caution, still turns in a miserably poor performance, the only conclusion must be that failure is the employee's fault. He just hasn't tried hard enough.

On that basis, explaining to the employee why you're 'going to have to let him go' can only be painful for both sides, and understandably most managers will dread it.

In contrast, however, great managers...

... understand that a person's talent and nontalent constitute an enduring pattern. They know that if, after pulling out all the stops to manage around his nontalents, an employee still underperforms, the most likely explanation is that his talents do not match his role. In the minds of great managers, consistent poor performance is not primarily a matter of weakness, stupidity, disobedience, or disrespect. It is a matter of miscasting.[6]

You can see how this way of framing the situation immediately closes the parity gap. There may still be no easy way to break the news, but there is a way of doing it that reduces collateral damage and allows the relationship to be maintained.

Relational Pensions

In 1831, two young men were sent to the United States by the French government to investigate the American prison system. Their names were Alexis de Tocqueville and Gustave de Beaumont. One product of the nine months they spent touring the country was de Toqueville's *Democracy in America*, an overview of America's society, economy and politics, still widely read for its clarity and remarkable foresight.

In the second volume, published in 1840, de Toqueville makes this observation:

> In America I saw the freest and most enlightened men placed in the happiest circumstances that the world affords; it seemed to me as if a cloud habitually hung upon their brow, and I thought them serious and almost sad, even in their pleasures.
>
> The chief reason for this contrast is that [they are] forever brooding over advantages they do not possess. It is strange to see with what feverish ardor the Americans pursue their own welfare, and to watch the vague dread that constantly torments them lest they should not have chosen the shortest path which may lead to it.
>
> A native of the United States clings to this world's goods as if he were certain never to die; and he is so hasty in grasping at all within his reach that one would suppose he was constantly afraid of not living long enough to enjoy them. He clutches everything, he holds nothing fast, but soon loosens his grasp to pursue fresh gratifications.
>
> In the United States a man builds a house in which to

spend his old age, and he sells it before the roof is on; he plants a garden and lets it just as the trees are coming into bearing; he brings a field into tillage and leaves other men to gather the crops; he embraces a profession and gives it up; he settles in a place, which he soon afterwards leaves to carry his changeable longings elsewhere. If his private affairs leave him any leisure, he instantly plunges into the vortex of politics; and if at the end of a year of unremitting labor he finds he has a few days' vacation, his eager curiosity whirls him over the vast extent of the United States, and he will travel fifteen hundred miles in a few days to shake off his happiness. Death at length overtakes him, but it is before he is weary of his bootless chase of that complete felicity which forever escapes him...

The recollection of the shortness of life is a constant spur to him. Besides the good things that he possesses, he every instant fancies a thousand others that death will prevent him from trying if he does not try them soon. This thought fills him with anxiety, fear, and regret and keeps his mind in ceaseless trepidation, which leads him perpetually to change his plans and his abode.

If in addition to the taste for physical well-being a social condition is added in which neither laws nor customs retain any person in his place, there is a great additional stimulant to this restlessness of temper. Men will then be seen continually to change their track for fear of missing the shortest cut to happiness.[1]

What de Toqueville noted as peculiar to the Unites States in 1840 is still recognizable today, both in the United States and in Europe, which has soaked up a lot of American influence through the international market economy.

In striking contrast to all this, a few years ago a friend was visiting a retail store based in Amritsar near New Delhi, India. He struck up a conversation with one of the numerous sales assistants – a teenager with an eager smile – and asked about his career plans. Did he want to set up his own business, or perhaps develop his career with larger retailers in nearby Delhi?

The young man looked perplexed. 'I am going to work here for the rest of my life,' he replied.

Movement is something Westerners take for granted. Geographical movement (commuting, moving house) and socio-economic movement (climbing the career ladder) appear to be two sides of the same coin.

In a culture driven mainly by financial objectives, this can make perfect sense. In relational terms, however, it may result in a kind of poverty of the most extreme kind.

Why do we have to keep moving?

Despite India's vast size and rapid economic development, life in much of it is still essentially local. You tend to live in the same place, doing the same thing, among the same people, till the end of your life. As a result, communities are very strong. There's a lot less money around, but there's a much richer social environment.

In countries such as the UK and the USA, most people have become used to something rather different. In the year 1998–99, 16 per cent of the US population moved home, 17.6 per cent of them to a different state.[2]

In a 2009 survey in the UK, over 2 million households had been resident at their current address for less than twelve months, and 3 per cent of house owners had moved. Among private renters, the proportion was 40 per cent.[3] Not all moves are long distance. According to a 2008 study, 58 per cent of households who moved in the previous three years found new accommodation within a five-mile radius.[4] But in comparison to a society such as India, there's a lot more churning in the form of population movement.

One prominent cause of migration in the UK is simply the breaking and reforming of households – between them accounting for 16 per cent of moves.[5] Another – more prevalent in the UK – is the effect of 'boarding school universities'. In countries such as France and Australia, most students attend nearby institutions and live at home to minimize accommodation costs. In the UK, however, the past system of maintenance grants has encouraged a different pattern. Students move to a different city to study and, not infrequently, stay there to work. In fact, in Sheffield an agency has been set up with the specific aim of 'capturing' graduates for Yorkshire companies, with a special focus on Sheffield's universities.

A more widespread influence, though, and one that's growing in importance with globalization, is that of the job market. Capital zips around the world so quickly now that demand for your particular skill may swiftly subside in one place and soar in another. Consequently, to get a better and higher-paying position – or perhaps just to get off unemployment benefits – you may find yourself moving from Seattle to Philadelphia, or from Newcastle to Swindon.

To some extent, job mobility has itself become a credential. There's currently an unwritten rule in London, for example, that real high-flyers won't stay in a job longer than three years. In addition, many corporations and public services still maintain a policy of 'training by moving around'. This is less marked than it was – partly because dual-income families are far harder to move. Nevertheless, there are organizations where it survives intact – not least in the UK's National Health Service.

Mobility: the downside

It's proverbially true that young single adults are less 'tied down' than older people with families. But this freedom exacts its own social cost. It often becomes necessary for a circle of friends to take on the supportive role otherwise performed by family (just look at the American comedy series *Friends*). But such a support network can be vulnerable in a move. Even your live-in partner will not always opt to sacrifice a job and go with you.

In contrast, migrants with families are able to carry their most supportive relationships around with them – at least in theory. But taking your spouse/partner and children with you in a move also spreads the problem around and creates other sources of stress – stress over new schools, lost friends, unfamiliar routines, difficulties for your partner in finding work.

And the likely effect is that your stress will be magnified by the stress of those close to you.

Does time heal? The answer is: yes, but only slowly. Social scientists estimate that it takes at least five years to integrate fully into a new area. If you move on before that time, you will be hard-pressed to form or sustain the kind of long-term relationships through which you can contribute significantly to, say, local politics, a parent and toddler group or a church.

Nor will short-term relationships be good for much in situations of real need. Talking over the fence with neighbours is one thing; getting help if you fall seriously ill or are bereaved is quite another. And in real life these things *can* suddenly happen.

Keeping your roots in a mobile society

It's important to balance things up here. After all, plenty of people negotiate changes of job and home without disaster. And a change of situation can – and should – be liberating, romantic, enlightening and stimulating. In addition, there are good reasons to move yourself *out* of familiar surroundings. The best opportunities in your line of work don't always pop up in the city where you happen to live. And travel does, after all, broaden the mind and deepen the experience.

For mobility to deliver those benefits, though, you need to keep in touch with your roots. Having roots isn't the same as being sedentary or stuck. It's having stability across a range of relationships from which you derive on-going emotional and practical support.

Long-standing communities tend to develop this naturally. It should not surprise us that, in an influential study of community in the USA, Robert Putnam concludes that:

> Social connectedness is a much stronger predictor of
> the perceived quality of life in a community than the

community's income or educational level. In the five communities surveyed having the highest social trust, 52 per cent of residents rated their community as an excellent place to live, the highest possible grade. In the five communities with the lowest levels of social trust, only 31 per cent felt that good about their quality of life. Similarly, personal happiness is also much more closely tied to the level of community social connectedness and trust than to income or educational levels... Even comparing two persons of identical income, education, race, age, and so on, the one living in a high social capital community typically reports greater personal happiness than his/her 'twin' living in a low social capital community.[6]

The challenge, in a mobile society that forces you to leave significant people behind, is to maintain your relational proximity even when you're on the move. In relationship terms, your roots will spread in many directions. Allowing for some overlap, there are seven main categories:

◆ home-sharing family (spouse/partner, children, parents, siblings)

◆ wider family (parents, grandparents, grown children, siblings, uncles and aunts)

◆ friends

◆ peers and colleagues

◆ mentors and teachers

◆ immediate neighbours

◆ local service providers.

Building roots requires ongoing two-way traffic in relationships, to the point where you enjoy a certain level of mutual trust. For

example, your mother can be relied on to look after your kids for
the weekend, just as you can be relied on to help with shopping
or clearing out the gutters. You establish strong enough links
with your neighbours that you can ask them to feed the cat
while you're on holiday. And so on.

Emotional support can be communicated quite effectively
without being geographically close. Phone, email, fast roads and
low airfares all help keep us 'in touch' without being permanently
close.

The greater challenge when you're mobile is to maintain
physical contact. Some forms of practical support rely heavily
on two bodies being in the same place – things like helping with
the decorating, walking the dog, going to the shops, getting to
a clinic.

Partly for this reason, a UK survey in 2004 found that 29 per
cent of employees would like to work from home on a regular
basis, with men and parents being the two groups of employees
most likely to have taken up offers from employers to work
from home.[7]

For the same reason, being physically present with colleagues
both helps their performance on the job and prevents them
from feeling marginalized. It's also true – particularly for older
people – that much of life's richness lies in being with family
and friends. The weekly phone call may not be enough to make
another person feel loved and supported, especially if the person
finds travel difficult and thus remains dependent on other
people's effort and initiative.

This is why retirement often presents you with a difficult
choice between staying where you've been living for the last ten
or twenty years – and thus where your friends are – or relocating
close to relatives (often children) and leaving your friends,
neighbours and familiar surroundings behind.

Putting down roots will almost inevitably involve tough
decisions about location. You don't have to stay in one town
from cradle to grave. But you have to be realistic about the
importance of location for your ability to maintain relationships,
and you may have to compromise creatively when work and
social relationships begin to pull you in opposite directions.

What is a relational pension?

Calum McBride manages one of Scotland's large department stores. But he feels he's in the wrong place. His elderly parents live in the south-east of England – some 400 miles away – and he wants to be close to them to give them the kind of support and help they need. Being based in Scotland makes fulfilling these family obligations extremely difficult. He now wishes, he says, that he had planned his career differently.

If he had only thought ahead and had foreseen the needs his parents would have at this stage of life, he could have planned his career within the store group so that he would have been working closer to them. When he was younger, however, he'd had no concept of roots and simply hadn't bothered to think about the long-term needs of his parents or other members of his family. The result was that he now felt guilty that he couldn't meet his parents' needs – despite the frustration and financial and time cost of trying to see them as much as he could.

Relationships, by nature, are long-term assets. You can offload them easily, but you can't buy them. Consequently, it's worth remembering that strategic decisions you make today will continue to have consequences for your relationships twenty, thirty and forty years down the line.

Commercials for pension funds usually push two messages. The first – explicitly the concern of the advertiser – is that, with the right kind of investment, you can enjoy a long, healthy and prosperous retirement. The second, almost always implicit, is that you have someone to share it with. Thus commercials of this kind routinely show a sprightly old couple enjoying the rewards of lifelong prudence *together*.

In reality, things are rather different. Prosperous or not, an enormous number of elderly people in the UK end up living on their own.

Overall, the trend has been away from family care and towards institutionalization. Partly, this reflects the pressures on women to contribute to household finances, leaving them less available to take up informal caring roles. In part, it's simple demographics.

An Australian researcher developed what he calls the *caretaker ratio* between the number of women aged fifty to sixty-four (often the prime caring group) and the number of persons aged eighty years and over. Projecting past trends, he estimated that the ratio would collapse dramatically by the year 2050, from 2.4 to 1 to around 0.8 to 1.[8]

On top of these factors, population mobility stretches relational distance and makes the practice of direct caring even more problematic. It's just a fact that, in a mobile society, the older members are the most likely to be neglected. And, sooner or later, that means you.

Some planners put faith in videoconferencing. 'Each Sunday I will be able to walk into my sitting room, switch on the equipment and have breakfast with my mother, even though we are 200 miles apart.'[9] If a disembodied breakfast meets your social needs, or your mother's, then fine. But probably it won't. And the only alternative to a relationally impoverished old age is to build the networks of contemporary and cross-generational relationships throughout your life that will sustain you in later years.

A relational pension – preparing for later years by building long-term relationships that will last into old age – may sound a strange device. And it could be argued that (life being what it is) relational pensions are vulnerable to outside forces, just as financial investments are affected by vagaries of the market. On the other hand, risk doesn't dampen our belief in saving. And relationships – carefully chosen, well spread and continually paid into – will usually offer impressive returns.

Relationships and health

Much stress arises through unsatisfactory relationships – between bosses and employees, between partners, between a person who wants affection and another who refuses to give it. And other channels of stress are relationship-connected – for example, work overload, time pressure, repetitive tasks and role conflict.

Major disorders resulting from stress include hypertension, coronary thrombosis, allergies, asthma, pruritus, peptic ulcers, constipation, rheumatoid arthritis, nervous dyspepsia, depression, diabetes, skin disorders and colitis.[10] Writing on emotional intelligence, Daniel Goleman points out that the link between stress and ill health now forms the basis of a leading medical subdiscipline called PNI, or psychoneuroimmunology.[11] Some of the main findings to emerge are these:

◆ **Stress taxes your body indirectly.** It's generally accepted that stress can make you eat too much, eat too little, hit the bottle or increase your consumption of cigarettes. But just as much damage is done when stress causes anger and aggression. An eight-year study of 1,012 heart-attack victims by Stanford University Medical School showed that aggressive men suffered the highest rates of second heart attacks. A Yale study of 929 men showed that those considered as easily roused to anger were three times more likely to die of cardiac arrest than those considered even-tempered. Anger and hostility, then, appear to be among the factors causing coronary artery disease.[12]

◆ **Stress lowers immune resistance.** A classic study by Sheldon Cohen of Carnegie Mellon University assessed the stress levels being experienced by a sample group and then exposed them all to the same strain of cold virus. He found that the people with the more stressed lives were more likely to catch the cold. Only 27 per cent of those with low stress levels caught the infection. Among those suffering high stress, the figure was 47 per cent. Comparable studies have shown that, for example, married couples who have gone through upsetting events such as marital fights were more likely to come down with a cold or upper respiratory infection.[13]

◆ **Isolation causes higher mortality rates**. Twenty-year studies involving 37,000 people indicate that social isolation – the sense that you have nobody to share your private feelings with or be close to – doubles your chances of sickness or death. In 1987, *Science* concluded that isolation was as significant to mortality rates as smoking, high blood pressure, high cholesterol, obesity and lack of physical exercise. In fact, social isolation is more likely to kill you than smoking.[14]

By contrast, you recover from illness faster and more fully when you have supportive relationships around you. The reasons aren't hard to work out.

First, relationships help you comply with your medical regime. Taking the tablets regularly, eating the right things and not 'overdoing it' are easier when somebody else is there to nag or encourage you. Second, being supported relationally plays a key role in boosting your morale and keeping depression at bay.[15] And third, other people are just an immense practical help. Your local doctor may prescribe rest, but you won't get much if there isn't somebody there to make your bed, cook your meals and assist with shopping.

A Swedish study published in 1993 examined the changing medical condition of 752 men as they aged from fifty-three to sixty. One striking discovery was that, although forty-one of the men died during the study period, among those who claimed to have a dependable network of close relationships – wife, close friends, children – there was no connection at all between high stress levels and death rate.[16] Close relationships, in other words, are good for health.

Similarly, there's a link between emotional support and resistance to cancer. Dr David Spiegel, of Stanford University Medical School, studied women with advanced metastatic breast cancer. Those who had nobody to unburden themselves to lived, on average, nineteen months after treatment. Those who joined weekly meetings with fellow women patients – meetings where they could speak freely about their fear, pain and anger, and be listened to – lived, on average, thirty-seven months. The difference could not be explained by any difference in medical treatment.[17]

Ways to implement relational pensions

A relational pension begins with being aware of the relationships through which most of the important business of your life is transacted – the relationships that form your 'relational base' as explored in the first chapter.

Usually, the more mobile you are, the harder it will be to maintain high levels of relational proximity with significant others. Also, the more mobile you are, the fewer significant others there are likely to be. If you want an instant snapshot of how strong your 'relational base' is, just ask yourself how many people you could call on for sustained help in the event of a crisis – say, a close family member falling ill.

You can't put down roots overnight. It takes time because building relationships takes time. But gradual investment over a period of years – meaning positive engagement in relationships as well as making good strategic decisions – will give you a store of relational wealth you cannot obtain in the short term.

1. When a job opportunity comes up, ask the strategic questions

Getting a new job and moving to new accommodation are both major life-changes. Making choices in these areas, we usually look at financial issues first: salary, purchase cost, terms and conditions, value for money, promotion prospects, investment potential and so on.

Planning a relational pension, however, directs attention to a different set of issues. It's clear that changes in work and housing have important implications for our relationships. Further, when we change job or move to a new house, we are in effect making strategic decisions with consequences that will follow us for years to come. It's worth getting them right.

◆ What benefits to my relationships are made possible by this increase in pay? Or, how might relational benefits outweigh the drop in salary?

◆ What will the location of the job, and its associated

travelling, do to my ability to maintain and build relationships that matter to me?

- ◆ What sort of relational environment does the job provide?

- ◆ What demands will the work make that may conflict with my commitment to relationships with my spouse/partner and family?

- ◆ Will I have sufficient support to cope with work-related stress?

- ◆ From the relationships point of view, is this job a step forward from my current position?

- ◆ Will taking this job entail disruption in the lives of those close to me – for instance, changes of school or employer?

- ◆ How will this move affect my distance from family and friends?

- ◆ How will the move affect my journey to work, and what consequences will this have for my relating time?

- ◆ How will the move affect others in the household – a partner in work, or children at school or playgroup?

- ◆ What kind of architectural environment am I moving into, and how will variables like number of bedrooms or garden affect relationships in the house?

- ◆ How close is the new accommodation to playgrounds, parks and other leisure facilities important to relaxation and relationship-building?

- ◆ If I have children, what quality of social environment does the neighbourhood provide? For instance, are there other children of comparable age?

◆ How easy will it be to maintain previous relationships, and what potential does the new location offer for forming new relationships?

◆ Is the local community receptive to incomers, or is the idyllic village likely to turn into a social nightmare?

◆ Are there facilities in the house for accommodating guests or having relatives to stay?

◆ Will I be well positioned when close members of my family might need my help, or I might need theirs?

◆ Will my children have the option of taking further education without being forced to leave home?

◆ Will both my partner and I be able to maintain and develop networks of significant social support?

◆ Is this a place where my children have the opportunity of working and settling within a reasonable distance?

There are some tough issues to face. For example, should you live near your side of the family or your partner's side? You might also ask whether it's worth trying to meet your potential neighbours before you commit to buying a house. Finding a mechanism for doing this isn't easy. Nevertheless, the position of your house determines to a large extent who it is you'll be mixing with in your local area. Just as important, if you have a family, it determines who it is your children will be mixing with.

2. Make the effort to connect

Time management coach Richard Winterton lives on the west side of Cambridge.

When a new couple moved in next door, Richard discussed with his wife whether or not they should make the effort of getting to know their new neighbours. In the end, they decided not to. Getting to know people is a time-consuming business. The chances were high that this new couple would themselves soon move on, after which the Wintertons would, in all probability, never see them again. So what was the point? As it happened, things turned out just as predicted. Two years later, the couple sold up and left.

However, when Richard later told this story in support of a point about time management, a Foreign Office representative took him to task. 'If everyone made that kind of calculation,' he said, 'the lives of many Foreign Office employees would be miserable. They would never develop friends. In the Foreign Office, you have to move every three years from one country to another. You rely heavily on people being willing to develop these short-term relationships in order to have any kind of quality of life.'

Most of us, seeing so many new faces day after day, just don't bother to make the effort with neighbours. One in three people living in the UK has never even met the person living next door.[18]

One advantage of moving, in relational terms, is that at least it offers the opportunity of a new start and new opportunities to connect. People with children sometimes have an advantage here, if only because the role of parent forces some new relationships on you – with school staff and other parents. But there are plenty of other ways to build new relationships.

Craig Newmark used to be the stereotypical geek: he even had glasses held together with Sellotape. Then when he moved to San Francisco, he got fed up with being lonely and began emailing his few acquaintances about upcoming events on the city's arts scene.

Six months later his 'list' had grown to 200, and soon 'Craig's List' became a kind of self-generating message board for Bay Area surfers.

The list finally turned into a group-run non-profit organization – 'an active source of support to the community... sponsoring training, mentoring, showcasing our community's talents, and giving other forms of help. We believe that the community members can help each other accomplish these changes, and we will facilitate those efforts.'[19]

Web-based interest groups have become a very successful source of social contacts – partly because search engines make it so easy to find other people who share your passion for off-road motoring or your challenges in coping with an autistic child. Similarly, many people use professional associations as a source of contact with other lawyers, accountants or architects.

Such networks vary in the degree to which they provide practical support. A friend who wanted to set up an English-language satellite link in the French Alps went on to the internet and found another expatriate who had done exactly the same thing. A brief exchange of emails saved a few hundred euros and a lot of time.

Many residential streets will house a staggering wealth of experience and technical expertise which could be tapped if only the individuals knew one another.

3. Don't waste relationships

Think back over the number of interesting introductions you've had – people you bumped into at social events, or on planes, and perhaps exchanged business cards with and said, 'Email me' or 'Give me a call'. How many of them did you mark on your relational base in the first chapter?

The fact is that most of us waste most of the relationship opportunities that come our way. And we do it in an age where keeping in touch is easier than it's ever been before.

Sometimes we go to a lot of trouble to develop relationships in one place and then simply 'lose touch' when we move somewhere else. Yet friendships represent a big investment. You wouldn't leave money behind. Why be ready to abandon close friends simply because you've changed jobs and relocated?

Try not to waste the 'bonding' experiences of working in the same firm or going to the same school or university. And if you've lost touch, try picking up the threads by using the website of an institution you used to belong to. The common experience of 'drifting apart' doesn't damage the friendship per se, but only prevents it from being pursued. Meet an old friend, and it's surprising how quickly you'll 'pick up where you left off', as long as the friendship had strong foundations.

Of course, the more people you know, the more urgently you will need to prioritize. You're unlikely to be able to keep more than 100 people on the list of those you contact at least once a month.

Finally, and perhaps most controversially, it's worth reflecting on the relational costs of divorce. Most decisions to divorce are made to secure greater current happiness. The financial consequences are well known. But divorcing your partner will drive a coach and horses through your relational pension, as it damages so many of your closest relationships and contacts with long-term friends.

4. Connect to the place you belong

Personal relationships aren't the only ones you can use to connect.

Consider all the links you have to your city and region. What are you doing to build the resources and the quality of life there?

For example, the UK charity City*life*, an offshoot of the Relationships Foundation, has pioneered the idea of employment bonds – a financial instrument that allows wealthier citizens or ex-citizens to lend money for a five-year term for socially productive purposes. For example, the capital sum is used for social housing or workspace development, where the construction labour is drawn as far as possible from the local unemployed, and the interest, forgone by investors, goes directly into local job creation initiatives.

Originally piloted in Sheffield, where the scheme raised almost £1 million, employment bonds have now been implemented in Newcastle upon Tyne, East London and Portsmouth, with similar schemes pending in areas as diverse as Cornwall, Hull, Medway, Nottingham and Glasgow.[20] Look out for opportunities like these for using your money to invest directly in your city. You may want also to give money to local charities that direct resources – human and financial – towards the disadvantaged in the city. Such schemes include not just helping the unemployed but benefiting the homeless and recycling urban waste.

It's also worth supporting local business. The prevalence of the word 'nearest' in online service locators such as the UK's upmystreet.com inevitably encourages the making of local connections. And local shops and services – the places you probably still depend on for your late-night pint of milk or Sunday papers – only remain within reach if you make a point of using them.

5. Think through the impact of your health on other people

Health isn't just a possession, an asset or a privilege; it's also a responsibility.

To some extent, this idea is embedded in the culture. Most of us were instructed as children to 'cover your mouth when you cough'. But we're far from consistent in applying the principle. In Japan, it's considered antisocial to travel on the Tokyo subway when you have a cold. In the UK – parental advice notwithstanding – it's macho to turn up at work even if you're running a temperature of 105.

A related area you may want to look at is taking a balanced approach to risk. For example, are you being fair to your partner or children if you fail to change your lifestyle after having a heart attack? Similarly – at a far earlier stage – where does the balance lie between the needs of those who depend on you and your own need to, say, work all hours, drink heavily, race motorcycles or go skydiving? The point is that personal lifestyle decisions have a relational angle. There's a place for risk-taking and living on the edge. There's also a place for making tomorrow's health needs register in today's decision-making. Reconciling the two is another aspect of self-management.

When other people depend on you, emotionally or financially, health is no longer simply 'your own business'. The woman whose husband is fifty-five, overweight and a heavy smoker has a right to feel her interests are being sidelined. He may be condemning her to spend her later years without the companionship and support she'd counted on.

6. Ask whose relational pension you are a part of

The point raised by the Foreign Office representative earlier opens up a wider question of how relational managers handle inductions and smooth the way for new employees to find their way into the team. New employees may need special attention in this respect. More widely, this chapter has approached relationship-building from the standpoint of someone thinking about his or her own future. But, in relational pensions, you are not just an investor; you are part of the investment. So it's worth reflecting on your obligations. Who has taken the trouble to invest relationally in you? And who, one day, will be relying on you for help and support?

CHAPTER 12

Relational Character

Business writer Dominic Laro tells the story of the night his wife almost died.

She had gone to the emergency department on a Saturday, suffering from a mild allergic reaction. They kept her in for observation. In the evening, he got a call from the intensive care unit, asking him to come in quickly. They'd discovered double pneumonia. Her allergies were preventing the use of the necessary antibiotics. They'd sedated and paralyzed her, and put her on a ventilator to force oxygen into her lungs. 'Come quickly' meant 'Be ready for the worst'.

He wrote later, 'Initially you don't believe it. How can someone you shared dinner with the night before be at the point of death? How can this clever, attractive, articulate woman be lying here, kept breathing by machines? And then you become, suddenly, vividly aware of the future. The emptiness. The children in the waiting room who think Mummy's coming home tomorrow. All the horrid, messy complications of life taking a lurch on to the dark side.'

There was nothing he could do. He took the children home, put them to bed and began what was, he said afterwards, the worst night of his life, praying that the phone would not ring.

It would be fatuous to draw from this story the moral that 'relationships matter'. Of course they matter. We all know they matter. Relationships – with family, friends, colleagues and community – matter in the way that health matters: as a precondition of well-being. Something you take for granted when you have it and miss desperately when it's gone.

What we have said in this book is that relationships matter

just as urgently in business. That things going right or wrong in business also have relational consequences. And – more cogently – that things going right or wrong in the relationships that comprise an organization, and link it to the world outside, will have clear business consequences – strategically, culturally, operationally and personally.

Consequently, there are tools available to relational managers that you do not pick up from business schools or from current definitions of 'best practice' in the organizational world. Some of them have been explored in this book.

But relational management does not easily reduce itself to a list of action points. It asks you not just what sort of things you do, but what kind of person you are trying to become. Anyone who spends significant time with you will be able to appreciate whether your actions are consistent, and therefore what underlying principles govern your life. It is this basic integrity – in the sense of being one consistent thing, not a contradiction of different things – that will determine how you influence others and what they remember you for. A good diagnostic question to ask is: 'If I lost my job tomorrow, and I no longer had the trappings and status of my office, what kind of person would I be?'

The relational manager is a relational person whether or not he's on a payroll. That's because almost every decision they make has significant relationship implications – whether it's in the workplace or out of it.

When Dominic Laro's wife got out of hospital ten days later, the family spent a long time discussing priorities. Their context was a busy dual-income household. You may be single, retired or separated, a lone parent or in a partnership without children. Whatever your situation, whatever your race, gender or sexual orientation, relational management confronts you with the same set of questions – not just how you want to operate professionally but what sort of life you want, what sort of values define you as a person, and what sort of society you play a part in building.

One way to approach this is to look at relational management on three levels.

Level one: Relational skills

Relational management can certainly be approached from the direction of cultivating relational skills – meaning cultural awareness, professional courtesy, sensitivity to others, the ability to listen. These traits are by no means as common in organizations as they ought to be. For example, a woman went into a UK branch of the NatWest to open a bank account and, in the course of being helped to fill out the form, was asked, 'Are you just a housewife?' She replied acidly, 'Are you just a bank clerk?'

This kind of inadvertent rudeness (and this is a mild example) inflicts real economic damage, both inside an organization and in its relations with clients and suppliers. That is why managers who know how to handle people, how to motivate and lead staff, will usually outperform those who don't.

Relational skills are a key issue in schooling, in management and in the constructive use of communications technology. People get more out of relationships if they know how to manage conflict without resorting to abuse or violence or withdrawal. Children learn these skills primarily at home, round the dinner table, in the give and take of family interaction.

The impact of this on business effectiveness two decades hence is one reason why companies should take more interest in the quality of workers' lives at home. Like it or not, most people don't just 'pick up' specific skills like self-disclosure, listening, commitment or self-representation – although employees often perform better when they go on relationship awareness courses.

Level two: Relational structures

Although it can be applied in any interaction, no matter how brief, deftness at relating is only the first level of relational management. A larger part consists of building relational proximity in relationships. An architectural analogy would be putting up the box girder framework on which to hang the walls, floors, power supply and plumbing. Without it, you won't get the building far off the ground.

With parity, for example, do you treat people on the basis of how powerful they are? Do you show the doorman the same respect as you show your board members? In principle, most business people would agree that this is a good thing to do; in practice, most of us breeze into the office without so much as a nod at the reception staff.

Or take connectivity. Roger Matthews is CEO of an IT company. He will talk to you enthusiastically about videoconferencing and how rapidly it's taking off. What he calls 'telepresence' enables companies to save huge amounts in transportation costs because executives no longer need to fly to meetings. But at what relational cost is this saving made? How effectively can relationships be built and maintained using only telepresence? And at an important meeting, just how effectively can you pick up signals from third parties? How much advantage do you lose just by limiting your capacity to read the meeting? There are arguments on both sides. The point is that few managers or executives seriously engage with the relational angle. And yet that relational angle may powerfully impact the bottom line.

Similar issues arise with time. In the twenty-first century, we take for granted our freedom to withdraw from relationships at relatively short notice. The commercial world is dominated by short-term contracts, the personal world by an expectation that friendships and child-raising partnerships will not necessarily be for life. We defend this right to opt out because we recall a time when getting out of commitments could be a great deal harder than getting in.

But keeping relational options open creates a different set of problems. Many of the benefits that good relating delivers to business and personal life – benefits based on mutual understanding, track record, empathy and trust, the products of relational proximity – occur more readily when relationships last.

Only in long-term relationships is there a sense of ongoing story of the kind that you have with the football club that you support. Memory plays a central role in this because relationships are not like marbles in a bag. They span time, overlap and overflow into each other, so that even remote memories passed down as stories in families and communities can continue to exert a powerful influence over present relationships.

There is even a sense in which organizations have memories – or don't. On your second call to a technical helpline, you will usually have to supply your case number, because you're now talking to a different operative. Without the case notes from your last call, the operative (and by extension the whole helpline desk) will have no memory of the previous conversation, and everything will have to be started afresh from scratch.

Level three: Relational ethos

Beneath the determination to build relational proximity is a third and deeper level which consists simply of a belief that relationships are intrinsically valuable.

This is such a basic observation that we are in danger of taking it for granted. We learn from our teachers, not just from our books. We secure the future well-being of our organizations by mentoring. And relationships dominate not just the mechanism of education but also the content. For while we train our children to set goals and seek excellence, we also impress on them the lessons of life, which are nearly always relational. We tell them that life is not just about maximizing earning power but about using their technical knowledge in a way that benefits others. And that values such as family, friendship, loyalty and love should be prized and protected.

In fact, if we wanted a single concept that made sense of the world, laid the foundations of character, helped us prioritize and gave us the tools to function effectively in management, that concept would surely focus on the word *relationships*.

The relational manager in the world

Relationships are falling more and more under the spotlight as an issue in social organization. Companies are increasingly recognizing internal and external relationships as the key to competitive advantage. Questions of how relationships should be regulated are also being discussed in the context of public service delivery in schools, hospitals and policing.

In other words, alongside the approach taken in this book – of individual relationship management – there is another approach of which the focus is public and organizational policy. And this is a thought to weigh carefully.

Take the Green Movement as an analogy. Just two years before her death in 1964, the ecologist Rachel Carson published *Silent Spring*. It was a revolutionary book because it was the first to bring to public attention the idea that industrial processes – such as the use of pesticides – could cause lasting damage to the environment.[1] Forty years later, green thinking has imprinted itself on our consciousness.

There is now a powerful political lobby representing environmental interests – meaning, broadly, the protection of the globe as a shared asset. And a sea change has taken place in the values that govern our behaviour. Individually, we recycle. Collectively, we haggle over global warming, biodiversity and deforestation.

Environmentalism is impeccably PC. It is a matter of direct self-interest. And it retains a kind of ethical purity, even if, in practice, it produces some tricky ethical dilemmas.[2] Saving the planet is a good we can all safely agree on.

But environmentalism has one odd feature. Although you will instinctively support the green agenda and may go to some trouble to put your old bottles in the right box, you probably won't have suffered any direct consequences of environmental change. The odds are against your having contracted cancer as a result of the hole in the ozone layer. Most people have yet to wade through an ocean oilspill. And, until recently, even global warming hasn't represented much more than a rising line on a graph.

By contrast, changes in social capital – in the overall quality of our relationships – have impacted on us constantly, and often severely. We moan, privately between ourselves and publicly in the media, about rising levels of violent crime, the spread of communicable diseases, misunderstandings in communication, endlessly growing pressure on our time and the uncertain future for our children. Relationships are the substance of our connection and the medium of our social ills. And yet, as a society, we simply haven't got to grips with the problem of relational breakdown.

The sociologist Robert Putnam has highlighted evidence of growing disconnectedness in Western societies, especially the USA. But without recasting issues of social capital as a relational issue, there is no obvious strategy – for individuals or for societies – to address the problem.

That's why relationships are not just a business issue but a social, economic and political issue. They provide a language in which we can address, debate and tackle the barriers that lie between us and the 'good society'.

They also underlie the entire environmental debate. Brazilian rainforests are bulldozed because the economic relationships between Western investors and logging companies take precedence over their social obligations towards those facing flooding as a result of global warming in Bangladesh. Whales flourish or are slaughtered, depending on whether we see our relationship with future generations as more, or less, important than the immediate relationships connecting commercial whalers to their markets. Relationships motivate conservation and exploitation.

Confronted with such global issues, most people will feel that the overall direction of trends isn't something they can do much about. Clearly, though, we don't take this rather limp attitude towards medical technology. We demand good physical health, and that demand translates into political commitment and public funding.

Why are we so supine when it comes to improving what is the key indicator of our personal happiness – the quality of our relationships? That is the main concern of the Relationships

Foundation, a Cambridge-based 'think and do tank' set up to examine the interplay of relationships and public policy.[3] If you're interested in this wider picture, you'll find plenty of material on the Relationships Foundation website (www. relationshipsfoundation.org), which demonstrates how to apply a relationships perspective to issues of public policy such as criminal justice, financial markets and health care provision.

Is this the proper concern of relational managers?

If all you take from this book is a few good ideas, then no. But if you understand the centrality of relationships in personal, business and global success, then the task of promoting and protecting good relationships will be on your agenda.

Ways to build relational character

1. Process situations relationally

There is a relational dimension to almost every situation we see. So, try observing what's happening relationally and thinking it through. For example, take the following situations (they're all real) and figure out what each is telling you about relationships and, specifically, about the connectedness, ongoing story, knowledge, respect/parity and common purpose between the players.

◆ You are leaving the office for an important meeting when the cleaner asks for a moment of your time. You're alert enough that you see anxiety in her face and register that the cleaner has never intercepted you like this before. But you're under a time crunch and, in corporate terms, the cleaner is not significant. What do you do?

◆ You've had an incredibly busy week. You're racing back home because you want to have dinner with your wife and three children, but you still haven't prepared your notes for tomorrow's sales presentation. On the fifteen-minute drive back from the station, do you run over the presentation in your mind or think about what you're going to talk about at the dinner table?

◆ It's the start of 2008 and you are a selector appointing a new coach for the Springboks. On the four-man shortlist are Peter de Villiers, the coach of the under-21 side; Heyneke Meyer, a former coach of the Pretoria-based Bulls Super 14 franchise; former South Africa assistant coach, Allister Coetzee; and former Super 12 Cats coach, Chester Williams. Who do you choose – and why? (If you want to test your selection against the choice of the South African Rugby Union, check out their decision on the internet.)

2. Devise a relational rule of life

No amount of reading about relationships will have much effect unless you consciously put it into practice.

One way of doing this is to incorporate relational thinking into your goal-setting. But the all-encompassing nature of your relationships makes goal-setting an unsuitable vehicle. So, what is proposed here is a rule of life.

The term *rule of life* will be familiar to anyone who's come across monastic orders, but the concept is not inherently religious. All it does is provide a code of principles that direct your actions. Anyone can have a rule of life, with any content, and it will benefit you in proportion to its ethical content and the discipline to live by it.

A relational rule of life is something everyone has to devise individually. As a starting point, we have decided to set one out for you on the next page. Consider how you might adapt it to your own life and circumstances.

In the end, bear in mind that it's your relationships that people will remember you for. The joke goes that pollster George Gallup had written on his tombstone, '84 per cent of people think I have gone to heaven.' Consider what you want written on yours. 'Great friend, wonderful partner, much-loved parent, respected colleague'? Or 'The executive who restructured his company three times in five years and thus sustained shareholder value through a difficult period in the markets'?

Tough choice?

A Relational Rule of Life

1. Process situations relationally.

Develop the habit of evaluating situations from a relational perspective.

2. Practise presence in your conversations.

Be totally present in your conversations. Avoid thinking forward to the next task or next conversation. Instead, enjoy the moment and engage with what's happening. Give feedback that assures the other person you're really listening.

3. Develop a story with everyone you meet.

Every relationship has its own special history. Make sure you review this and plan constructively. Where has the relationship gone up to now? Where are you hoping it will go in the future?

4. Cultivate relational intelligence.

Be aware of what others are thinking and feeling. Read and interpret the signals. Is a person accepting what you're saying? Are they acting on instructions? If not, why not? What's going on relationally when you interact?

5. Find ways of closing the parity gap.

Subtle power differentials – physical, financial, reputational – can be at play and make a powerful impact on a relationship without you being aware of it. Do you find yourself compensating when you interact with someone younger, poorer, smaller, of a different gender or in a wheelchair?

6. Gather information about others and retain it.

Deliberately broaden your knowledge of other people or organizations. Fill in the blanks in your knowledge so you get a well-rounded picture. Register and evaluate information that comes to you from third parties. And make sure you remember it.

7. Think from the other side.

The person who calls you only when they need something does not appreciate the need for shared objectives. Ensure that your conversations with others are mutually beneficial and that both sides have an incentive to continue the relationship and profit from it. If the relationship matters, call even if you have nothing you need to ask for.

8. Take time to plan your day relationally.

What are the key relationships on your timetable? Take a few minutes every morning to think over who you are going to meet and how that meeting will build that relationship. Cultivate a sense of caring for the other person by reviewing their situation in advance. Is a phone call good enough or do you really need to go in person?

9. Do a relational evaluation.

This is a self-correcting process. At the end of the day, take a few moments to review what's happened in your relationships. Have your conversations gone badly or well, and what can you learn from that? If you want, make this an exercise in diary-keeping.

10. Value relationships above everything else.

What is the most important thing in your life? If you say 'My car', you probably need a psychotherapist! The reality is that we do value relationships above everything. The challenge for most of us is to keep it in mind in the crucible of commercial competition.

Notes

Chapter 1

1. *Fortune*, 22 June 1998.
2. We are indebted to Mr Paul Sandham of Sandham Associates for applying relational thinking to this area.
3. Robert Waterman, *The Frontiers of Excellence: Learning from Companies that Put People First*, London: Nicholas Brealey, 1994, p. 170.
4. See Arlie Russell Hochschild, *The Time Bind: When Work Becomes Home and Home Becomes Work*, Second Owl Books, 2001, p. 19.
5. Daniel Roth, 'My Job At The Container Store' in *Fortune*, 10 January 2000.
6. Nicholas Stein, 'Winning the War to Keep Top Talent' in *Fortune*, 29 May 2000.
7. J. H. Oldham, *Real Life Is Meeting*, London: Sheldon Press, 1958.

Chapter 2

1. RSA Inquiry, *Tomorrow's Company: The role of business in a changing world*, London: RSA, 1995, p. 11.
2. See Michael Schluter and David Lee, *The R Factor*, London: Hodder & Stoughton, 1993. A wide range of literature on relational issues can be obtained on the Relationships Foundation website: www.relationshipsfoundation.org
3. Alison Maitland, 'Chats over coffee hard to replace', *Financial Times*, 8 May 2000, p. 34.
4. Damage caused by losing employees can be severe. According to John Challenger, CEO of outplacement firm Challenger Gray & Christmas, 'Companies now face the most competitive job market in decades, and losing workers can savage a bottom line. When you consider lost productivity and replacement costs, a single defection can cost a company between $50,000 and $100,000. It gets even worse if you lose top talent, with their vast stores of intellectual capital gleaned over years at the company. Knowing how to retain top people in this challenging environment can be a real competitive advantage.' Quoted by Nicholas Stein, 'Winning the War to Keep Top Talent' in *Fortune*, 29 May 2000.
5. *Financial Times*, 26 July 2000. Note that, according to the US Census Bureau, over half (56.4 per cent) of all US employees have been in their current jobs less than four years. For workers age 25–34, the figure rises to 69.2 per cent. See: *Statistical Abstract of the United States, 2000, No. 664*: 'Distribution of workers by tenure with current employer, 1998'.
6. See www.cfsv.org/communitysurvey. If anything, the situation seems to be worse in the UK, where the Industrial Society has discovered that 93 per cent of managers do not trust their employees (*Financial Times*, 26 July 2000. Article by Will Hutton and John Knell, 'A new network economy is breeding a less loyal

and more independent worker'. Inside Track – Born Free – Viewpoint).

7. At W. L. Gore, the American company better known as the maker of Gore-Tex® fabric and Elixir guitar strings, procedural fairness with a strong relational element is practised in remunerating and rewarding employees, who are all known as 'associates'. Compensation is determined by a lengthy and complex process that incorporates rankings from one's own team members and the decisions of a compensation committee. Information about how pay decisions are made based on consistent processes is openly shared. Such procedural fairness has undoubtedly helped create a strong sense of commitment among employees. One receptionist said she would work there for minimum wage. M. Weinreb, 'Power to the People' in *Sales & Marketing Management*, April, pp. 30–35.

8. This is less true in company structures outside the PLC. In the John Lewis Partnership, for example, even the checkout staff are partners in the ownership of the company and have a say in its management.

9. Lisa Hoecklin, *Managing Cultural Differences: Strategies for Competitive Advantage*, Wokingham, England: Addison-Wesley, 1995, p. 117.

Chapter 3

1. For American readers, the total bill was a little over a dime.

2. See, for example, Rebecca O'Neill, *Experiments in Living: The Fatherless Father*, Civitas, September 2002, available at www.civitas.org.uk. Also Michael Argyle's excellent summary, 'The effects of relationships on wellbeing' in Nicola Baker (ed.), *Building a Relational Society*, Aldershot: Arena, 1996, p. 43.

3. The impact of relationships on personality formation has long been accepted by psychiatrists. See Henry Stack Sullivan, *The Interpersonal Theory of Psychiatry* edited by H. S. Perry and M. L. Gawel, New York: Norton, 1953.

4. Quoted in *The Week*, 9 December 2000, p. 12.

5. See Arlie Bussell Hochschild, *The Time Bind: When Work Becomes Home and Home Becomes Work*, Second Owl Books, 2001, p. 46.

6. See 'Leadership by example not rhetoric' in *Financial Times*, 8 May 2000, p. 35.

7. Tom Peters, *Liberation Management: Necessary Disorganization for the Nanosecond Nineties*, London: Macmillan, 1992, p. 366.

8. *Guardian*, 5 March 2001.

9. See 'The strains of juggling home and work', *Financial Times*, 8 May 2000, p. 34.

10. See IT Review, *Financial Times*, 1 December 1999, p. 3.

Chapter 4

1. See BBC report at: www.bbc.co.uk/blogs/technology/2009/02/facebook_still_showing_growing.html.

2. Jonathan Winter and Charles Jackson, *The Conversation Gap: Using Dialogue to Build Trust and Inspire Performance*, Career Innovation, 2004.

3. Jan English-Lueck, *Technology and Social Change: The Effects on Family and Community*, an address to the COSSA Congressional Seminar, 19 June 1998.

4. This and following quote from Howard Rheingold, 'Look Who's Talking' in *Wired*, January 1999.

5. In the UK, for example, a recent NOP survey showed that by the beginning of 2001, half of all children aged 7–16 possessed a mobile phone. By the same

point, 85 per cent of those aged 16–24 had accessed the internet (up from 69 per cent in July 2000). Home internet usage in the UK quadrupled in the last four years of the twentieth century.
6. See BBC news item: http://news.bbc.co.uk/2/hi/uk_news/england/essex/4749099.stm
7. M. Weinreb, 'Power to the People' in *Sales & Marketing Management*, April 2003, pp. 30–35.
8. See: www.gore.com/en_xx/aboutus/fastfacts/index.html
9. Even letters of complaint are apt to begin with 'Dear Sir/Madam' – one of a range of mechanisms limiting the damage the content of a letter can do to the writer's relationship with the recipient. By contrast, email currently relies on emoticons or slightly ambiguous mood symbols such as (J or :-) for 'happy' and >:-O for 'angry and shouting'.
10. See http://www.management-issues.com/2006/8/24/research/e-mail-bullying-on-the-rise.asp
11. B. B. Baltes, M. W. Dickson, M. P. Sherman, C. C. Bauer and J. LaGanke, 'Computer-mediated communication and group decision making: a meta-analysis' in *Organizational Behavior and Human Decision Processes*, January 2002, pp. 156–79.
12. Reported by Andy Hobsbawm, 'Visual Anonymity' in *Financial Times*, 29 April 2000.
13. Robert Kraut, Michael Patterson, Vicki Lundmark, Sara Kriesler, Tridas Mukopadhyay and William Scherlis, of Carnegie Mellon University, 'Internet Paradox: A social technology that reduces social involvement and psychological wellbeing?' in *American Psychologist*, Vol. 53, No. 9, pp. 1017–31, September 1998.
14. http://www.uoguelph.ca/news/2009/02/post_176.html
15. Source: Professor Paul Ekman in the BBC programme *About Face*, broadcast 2001.

Chapter 5

1. See: www.telegraph.co.uk/news/newstopics/politics/lawandorder/4932844/City-boss-gave-bigger-bonuses-to-employees-he-slept-with-tribunal-hears.html
2. From Spike Milligan, *Puckoon*, 1963.
3. The annual report 2000 for British supermarket giant Tesco shows Mr T. P. Leahy's total package as £1,173,000. According to a report from the Incomes Data Services, September 1999, quoted by Unison, a sales assistant earns an average of £5.16 an hour. Based on a 35-hour week, 52-week year, this comes to £9,391 a year – 0.8 per cent of the CEO's package – although other elements may make up the sales assistant's total package.
4. Nassim Nicholas Taleb, 'How bank bonuses let us all down' in *Financial Times*, 24 February 2009.
5. According to the US Census Bureau (*Statistical Abstract of the United States 2000*), 67.5 per cent of American families have a credit card. Of these, 46.3 per cent – almost half – only 'sometimes' or 'hardly ever' pay off the balance at the end of the month. According to NOP, 'In 2001, 45% of the UK adult population have a credit card. Before the wave of competition that hit the industry in 1994, the penetration rate was only 32%' (NOP Financial Research Survey, May 2001 and NOP Financial Research Survey 1994/95). 'Taking an average of the first six months of 2001, roughly 50% of Barclaycard's credit card customers paid interest (or borrowed) and did not pay their balance in full. This figure has remained stable in recent years' (Source: Barclaycard internal statistics).
6. Andrew Hartropp (ed.), *Families in Debt*, Jubilee Centre Research Paper No.

7, Cambridge: Jubilee Centre Publications, 1987, p. 57.
7. In the USA, statistics show that as many as 70 per cent of divorcing couples attribute the breakdown of their marriage to arguments about finances. See *State of California Employee Assistance Programme Newsletter*, Vol. 5, No. 8, February 1999.
8. See Geraint John, 'The Toyota Way' in *The CPO Agenda*, Spring 2007.

Chapter 6

1. Marcus Buckingham and Curt Coffman, *First, Break All the Rules: What the World's Greatest Managers Do Differently*, London: Simon & Schuster, 1999, p. 33.
2. David Molpus: *Who's The Worst Boss?* radio broadcast, 18 June 2002, reported at: http://www.npr.org/programs/morning/features/2002/june/bosses/index.html
3. Edgar H. Schein, *Organizational Culture and Leadership*, London: John Wiley & Sons, 2004.
4. Reported by Edward M. Hallowell, 'The Human Moment at Work' in *Harvard Business Review*, January–February 1999.
5. See: www.hughpearman.com/articles/cwa8b.htm
6. See: www.hughpearman.com/articles/cwa8b.htm
7. T. H. Davenport and L. Prusak, *Working Knowledge: How Organizations Manage What They Know*, Cambridge, MA: Harvard Business School Press, 1980.
8. See: http://news.bbc.co.uk/2/hi/uk_news/magazine/7914698.stm
9. See: http://news.bbc.co.uk/2/hi/uk_news/magazine/7914698.stm
10. Marcus Buckingham and Curt Coffman, *First, Break All the Rules: What the World's Greatest Managers Do Differently*, London: Simon & Schuster, 1999, p. 28.
11. See Michael Argyle, 'The effects of relationships on wellbeing' in Nicola Baker (ed.), *Building a Relational Society*, Aldershot: Arena, 1996, p. 41.
12. Industrial Society, *New Community or New Slavery? The Emotional Division of Labour*, published 22 November 2000.
13. See: http://business.timesonline.co.uk/tol/business/related_reports/business_solutions/article5308916.ece
14. Howard Berkes, *CEO's Resignation Punctuates Turmoil at Red Cross* (http://www.npr.org/templates/story/story.php?storyId=16747746&ft=1&f=1001).
15. C. S. Lewis, *The Four Loves*, London: Fontana, 1960, p. 66.
16. Theodore E. Zorn, 'Bosses and Buddies: Constructing and Performing Simultaneously Hierarchical and Close Friendship Relationships' in Julia T. Wood and Steve Duck, *Under-studied Relationships*, California: Sage, 1995, p. 140.
17. John Ashcroft, 'Corporate Hospitality', unpublished paper, November 1998, the Relationships Foundation.

Chapter 7

1. *Leaders for Today*, 2006, No. 3, p. 21.
2. Healthcare Commission, *Investigation into Mid Staffordshire NHS Foundation Trust*, London: Healthcare Commission, 2009.
3. Quoted by Enrico Grazzini in *Intervista a Tim Berners-Lee, l'inventore del WWW*, 7 May 2008 (http://nuovo.enricograzzini.it/?p=74).
4. See: www.tomnewsom.com/site_files/atticus/Atticus_entry.pdf

5. See: www.tomnewsom.com/site_files/atticus/Atticus_entry.pdf
6. Clive Woodward, communicated at a public lecture.

Chapter 8

1. *An Unexpected Tragedy: Evidence for the connection between working patterns and family breakdown in Australia*, Australia: Relationships Forum Australia, 2007, p. 31.
2. According to an IPD survey, 'Two-fifths [of respondents] report that working long hours has resulted in arguments with their spouse or partner... Nearly a third admit that work-related tiredness is causing their sex life to suffer, and 42% say that friendships have been damaged.' Reported in the *Guardian*, 5 March 2001.
3. Taken from Bluewater's website at www.bluewater.co.uk
4. Figures from the US Census Bureau, decennial census and American Community Survey, as reported by the Population Reference Bureau, www.prb.org/Articles/2008/commuting.aspx
5. As reported by the BBC: http://news.bbc.co.uk/2/hi/uk_news/education/4669378.stm
6. Figures from the Stanford Institute for the Quantitative Study of Society in America. See Cherry Norton, 'Even moderate surfing harms your social life', *Independent*, 28 February 2000.
7. Diane Appleyard, 'TV Cold Turkey', *FEMAIL Forum (Daily Mail)*, 17 December 1998.
8. Louis de Bernières, *Captain Corelli's Mandolin*, London: Minerva, 1995, p. 281.
9. See *APA Monitor*, 28 (10), 8, October 1997.
10. M. W. Gillman, S. L. Rifas-Shiman, et al., 'Family dinner and diet duality among older children and adolescents', *Archives of Family Medicine* 9, pp. 235–40 (2000).
11. See *Daily Telegraph*, 3 April 2001.
12. Cited by Virginia Ironside, *Independent*, 27 October 1995.
13. The UK is far ahead of its European partners in encouraging Sunday working. In 1999, 39 per cent of UK employees did Sunday work. This contrasts with 23 per cent in Germany, 25 per cent in France and 15 per cent in Spain. Source: Eurostat 2000.
14. In many sectors, good employees are scarcer than jobs. Among the USA's top employers, for example, 83 per cent offer bounties to employees for recommending new hires. See Robert Levering and Milton Moskowitz, 'America's Top Employers' in *Fortune*, 8 January 2001.
15. Note, for instance, that in the UK one in five children suffers stress-related illnesses which are linked to the long hours worked by their parents (*Guardian*, 17 April 2000).
16. Quoted by Theodore Zeldin, *Conversation*, London: Harvill Press, 1998, p. 33.
17. Theodore Zeldin, *Conversation*, London: Harvill Press, 1998, p. 46.

Chapter 9

1. In the USA, there would be a reason for this, since anyone attempting to assist an accident victim might later be sued if his efforts could be shown to have worsened the victim's condition.

2. From John Edmund Haggai, *The Influential Leader: Twelve Steps to Igniting Visionary Decision Making*, Grand Rapids: Harvest House, 2009.

Chapter 10

1. See: *My boss is talking about me to everyone!* OfficePolitics.com, 9 January 2009 (http://www.officepolitics.com/advice/?p=373).
2. Donald W. Shriver Jr, *An Ethic for Enemies: Forgiveness in Politics*, New York: Oxford University Press, 1995, p. 6.
3. Rich DeVos, *Ten Powerful Phrases for Positive People*, New York: Hachette Book Group, 2008.
4. Quoted in David Augsburger, *Caring Enough to Forgive – Caring Enough to Not Forgive*, California: Regal Books, 1981, p. 13.1. Reported in the *Guardian*, 8 January 2000.
5. Quoted by Trudy Grovier, 'Forgiveness and the Unforgivable' in *American Philosophical Quarterly*, Vol. 36, No. 1, January 1999, p. 64.
6. Marcus Buckingham and Curt Coffman, *First, Break All the Rules: What the World's Greatest Managers Do Differently*, London: Simon & Schuster, 1999, p. 209.

Chapter 11

1. Alexis de Tocqueville, *Democracy in America*, Vol. 2, Bk 2, Ch. 13, ed. Phillips Bradley, New York: Vintage Books, 1990, p. 8, quoted in Dale S. Kuehne, *Sex and the iWorld: Rethinking Relationship beyond an Age of Individualism*, Grand Rapids: Baker Academic, 2009.
2. Source: *US Census*, Current Population Reports: Geographical Mobility (Update) March 1998 to March 1999, at: http://www.census.gov/prod/2000pubs/p20-531.pdf
3. Source: DCLG (2009), *Housing Surveys Bulletin, Issue Number 4*, London: Department for Communities and Local Government.
4. Source: DCLG (2008), *Housing in England 2006/07*, London: Department for Communities and Local Government.
5. Source: *Social Trends 2001*, Table 10–17, p. 185.
6. See Robert D. Putnam, *Bowling Alone: Collapse and Revival of American Community*, New York: Simon & Schuster, 2000. Much of the data behind the book is available on the website: www.bettertogether.org
7. See J. Stevens, J. Brown and C. Lee, *The Second Work–Life Balance Study: Results from the Employees' Survey*, London: Department of Trade and Industry, 2004.
8. *Who's going to care? Informal care and an ageing population, Report prepared for Carers Australia by the National Centre for Social and Economic Modelling*, University of Canberra: NATSEM, 2004, p. 12. It should be noted that the ratio is a fairly crude indicator that ignores intra-generational caring and finer definitions of need.
9. See Michael Moynagh and Richard Worsley, *Understanding the Present by Thinking about the Future*, London: The Tomorrow Project, 2000, p. 97.
10. See Jill Earnshaw and Cary Cooper, *Stress and Employer Liability*, London: Institute of Personnel and Development, 1996, Table 2, p. 9.
11. Daniel Goleman, *Emotional Intelligence: Why It Can Matter More Than IQ*, London: Bloomsbury, 1996, p. 167.
12. See Lynda H. Powell, 'Emotional Arousal as a Predictor of Long-Term

Mortality and Morbidity in Post M.I. Men' in *Circulation*, Vol. 82, No. 4, Supplement III, October 1990, p. 259.
13. See Sheldon Cohen et al., 'Psychological Stress and Susceptibility to the Common Cold' in *New England Journal of Medicine*, 325 (1991). Also: Arthur Stone et al., 'Secretory IgA as a Measure of Immunocompetence' in *Journal of Human Stress*, 13, 1987.
14. The difference in mortality risk is 2.0 to 1.6. See James House et al., 'Social Relationships and Health' in *Science*, 29 July 1988.
15. Prevalence of treated depression in the UK is relatively low – around 3 per cent for men, and 7.5 per cent for women (source: NHS General Practice Statistics on www.statistics.gov.uk). However, NHS Direct estimates that, at any one time in the UK, depression affects about 15–30 per cent of people. Over a lifetime, there is a 60–70 per cent chance that you will suffer depression that affects your daily living. This effect is reinforced by medical advances and improvements in living standards, which reduce the impact of physical illnesses like pneumonia and thus cause the relative impact of depression to increase. Depression is already ten times more common in the USA than it was two generations ago (source: Robert Putnam in *Le Monde*, quoted in *The Week*, 9 December 2000). It is estimated that by the year 2020 depression will be the second most common cause of disability in the developed world and the prime cause in the developing world.
16. See Annika Rosengren et al., 'Stressful Life Events, Social Support, and Mortality in Men Born in 1933' in *British Medical Journal*, 19 October 1993.
17. See David Spiegel et al., 'Effect of Psychosocial Treatment on Survival of Patients with Metastatic Breast Cancer' in *Lancet*, No. 8668, ii, 1989.
18. Statistic from the *Sunday Times*, quoted in *The Week*, 23 December 2000, p. 22.
19. Reported in *R Briefing*, Issue 23. Available from the Relationships Foundation.
20. For further information, visit the City*life* website: www. relationshipsfoundation.org/citylife/Index.html. 8 See the full case study at: www.celltd.demon.co.uk/study.htm. 9 This organization was set up through the Episcopal Church of Scotland, and can be contacted via the church office in Edinburgh.

Chapter 12

1. Rachel Carson, *Silent Spring*, Boston: Houghton Mifflin Company, 1962.
2. Which, for example, is more important – jobs in the fishing industry, or preservation of stocks of North Sea cod?
3. Michael Schluter and David Lee, *The R Factor*, London: Hodder & Stoughton, 1993. See particularly p. 68ff. Copies of *The R Factor* can be ordered directly from the Relationships Foundation or through its secure website: www. relationshipsfoundation.org/books/Index.html

RELATIONSHIPS FOUNDATION

VISIT OUR WEBSITE
www.relationshipsfoundation.org

To:

☑ Join the Relationships Foundation's free mailing list and receive its regular briefings

☑ Find out more about the Foundation's work

☑ Access its resources on assessing relationships

☑ Order its books

☑ Make a financial contribution if you would like to support its work

The Relationships Foundation
3 Hooper Street
Cambridge
CB1 2NZ

Tel: +44 (0)1223 566333

RELATIONSHIPS GLOBAL

A consequence of the information technology revolution and globalization has been to connect people across the globe; but at the same time the huge increase in mobility and demands on our time are a threat to community and close and intimate relationships.

To counteract the many negative forces undermining relationships in all societies today, the Relationships Foundation in the UK and Relationships Forum Australia have started to lay out what a national policy framework might look like if based on a relational approach. This has included defining a new goal for public policy (to replace the narrow focus on economic growth), new goals for public services (health, education and criminal justice) and changes in the goals and structure of public and private companies.

Since 1993 the Relationships Foundation has been developing a new set of metrics to be able to assess quality of relationships within and between organizations. This has been applied in a wide range of organizational contexts in the UK, including companies, primary healthcare, homes for older people, the prison system and non-profit organizations.

Taken together, these developments offer the possibility of a new relational framework for public policy and the business world, which we have called 'Relational Thinking'.

Relationships Global has been established as an international network of organizations and individuals who recognize the importance of relationships for human wellbeing and who care enough to get involved in building a more relational world.

If you would like to become part of this network, on behalf of an organization or as an individual, please visit our website: **www.relationshipsglobal.net**